This book belongs

_____
Name

_____   _____
Phone 1:   Phone 2:

_____   _____
Health Insurance Co. and Policy Number: Doctor/Midwife:

_____   _____
Address   Phone:

Baby:

_____   _____
Name: Pediatrician Name/number:

_____   _____
Date of birth: Baby's Health Insurance Co.
and Policy Number:

In case of emergency:

_____   _____
Name: Name:

_____   _____
Phone 1/Phone 2:   Phone 1/Phone 2:

Important Contacts:

_____   _____
Name: Name:

_____   _____
Phone 1/Phone 2:   Phone 1/Phone 2:

For my mother and father,

with love and gratitude

The Baby File

All the Lists, Forms, and Practical Information You Need

Before and After Baby's Arrival

RUNNING PRESS
PHILADELPHIA · LONDON

Printed in China

This book is meant to be used a workbook, and parts of it can be photocopied for personal use—but not for resell or distribution. All websites mentioned within the book are listed as informational resources, but are not endorsed by the publisher.

The Postpartum Plan may be copied and distributed without further permission, on the condition that it is not used in any context which violates the WHO code on the marketing of breastmilk substitutes.

9 8 7 6 5 4 3 2 1
Digit on the right indicates the number of this printing

Library of Congress Control Number:2007938921

ISBN 978-0-7624-2735-2

Cover design by Maria Taffera Lewis
Interior design by Maria Taffera Lewis
Typography: Avenir, Garamond, and Bradley Hand ITC

This book may be ordered by mail from the publisher.
Please include $2.50 for postage and handling.
But try your bookstore first!

Running Press Book Publishers
2300 Chestnut Street
Philadelphia, PA 19103-4371

Visit us on the web!
www.runningpress.com

Table of Contents

Part III - Looking Ahead

Chapter 6: Childcare

Chapter 7:
Family Financial Matters

Appendix

Introduction

Congratulations! If you're reading this, you are either expecting a baby or welcoming a baby into your life. Parenthood affects everyone differently, and one of the many changes for me was an undeniable urge to write this book. Of course The Baby File did not start out as a book. When I was pregnant, I noticed post-it notes proliferating around my house. These notes contained important information—the number for a pediatrician recommended by a friend, my company's benefits website, an abbreviated list of favorite baby names. . . . the list goes on.

I was appalled by my own lack of organization (and I was to be somebody's mother!) As you might have predicted, the situation with the post-its did not improve after my daughter, Julia, was born. There was now a whole other person to care for, with her own array of facts and figures. Julia didn't gain back her birthweight as quickly as our pediatrician would have liked, so right off-the-bat there was a lot of recording of feeding times, tallying of dirty diapers, and weighing—all of which had to be organized in some way.

To be sure, in my postpartum haze I did not create worksheets. But what I struggled with in those early weeks later became the worksheets in this book. Because I know that every baby brings his or her own set of circumstances, I started asking other moms what kind of information they needed to retain and organize, when their kids were born. And ultimately, those conversations were the basis for the topics included in this book.

Now that you have an idea of why I put these resources together, you might be saying to yourself, "OK, but how do I use this book? How will it save me time—me who cannot even steal a moment to brush my teeth today, me with the dark circles under my eyes and the stack of dishes in the sink?" Unfortunately, this book will not do your laundry, write your thank-you notes, or improve your personal hygiene. But what it will do is demystify some parenting concepts and allow you to find answers to your questions quickly. If the answer you seek is not in this book, there are lists of resources on every topic included at the end of each section or chapter. Just flip through to your topic *du jour*. Baby has a rash and you think it could be a reaction to something you ate? Use the Food intake worksheet to figure it out. Everyone keeps saying the words "attachment parenting" and you haven't a clue? See the Sleep chapter, which compares attachment parenting with other philosophies of care.

Finally, I hope this book will offer you a welcome dose of humor or empathy when you need it most. I hope it will assure you that even though we're all hunkered down as new parents, trying to adjust to our new lives, you are now a proud, card-carrying member of the sleepy-eyed, hard-working, love-crazed parent club.

Amanda Dobbins

Bio:

Amanda lives near Boston with her husband and two children. She has worked in educational publishing for ten years. Amanda's writing has appeared in *Parenting Magazine, The Baby File* is her first book.

Acknowledgments:

There is a proverb that says birth is ultimately a journey a woman walks alone. Fortunately for me, writing a book was not. As The Baby File makes its appearance I feel extremely grateful to have had so much guidance and encouragement.

Thank you to the San Francisco Public Library and librarians, not only for providing me a peaceful place to work, but also offering most of the resources I needed to put this book together.

I owe much of my enthusiasm for writing to Geoff Marchant at Hotchkiss. I am indebted to him for the discipline of daily themes and for affirming the idea that I could write.

Thank you to the great team at Running Press for taking a chance on this project. For being early champions of *The Baby File* and encouraging me to try, try again, thank you J. McCrary and Deb Grandinetti. Special thanks to Jennifer Kasius for her unflagging enthusiasm and for relating to this book on a personal level as well.

The Baby File is much enhanced by the opinions and experiences of everyone who agreed to be interviewed, sharing the perspective of moms who are artists, executives and business owners, a Doula/Psychotherapist, and a Pediatrician. Thank you Maria Burtis, Sylvia Herrera-Alaniz, Carrie White, Margaret Bergmann-Ness, and Dr. Will Wilkoff.

Julie Bouchet Horwitz talked with me at length about the Postpartum Plan she developed and gave permission for her calendar and concept to be printed in *The Baby File*. I know she did so in the interest of reaching and serving more moms and it's nice to know we're all on the same team.

A huge thank you to my friends who tirelessly answered questions about everything from setting up a nursery to estate planning. I am grateful to everyone who contributed, but especially to Gwen Dumont, Danielle Meagher, Eliza Phillips, Angela Kalayjian, Erika Kelly, Liz McArthur, Bryony Gagan, Michele Friedman, Amy Sanders, Gage Dobbins and Gerry Rigby for reading early drafts and giving my research so much thought and attention. Your insight and suggestions have been crucial to this project.

I've been grateful every day of my parenting life to the amazing women who have helped care for Julia and Charles: Angelina Beniflah, Viviane Rosenberg, Pilar Teso. To everyone at Angelina's, thank you for taking such great care of Julia and helping her through so many early milestones. A very special thank you to Ana America Crespin. Your kindness and dedication to our children have been an incredible blessing for our family.

Thank you to my brother, Alex, for your encouragement throughout this project. I loved strategizing with you. Our relationship is a great source of inspiration for me as I do my best to help Julia and Charles build the kind of sibling bond we share.

My mother and father have each been and continue to be role models for me and it is a wonderful feeling to want to emulate your own parents. I thank my Dad for his support along every path I've pursued and more recently for his help along the publishing path. I appreciate your quiet, steady reassurance and your pride in me. No matter my age, hearing that you are proud of me and my accomplishments does not lose its importance.

I am profoundly grateful to my mother who has supported me in every possible sense of the word throughout two pregnancies, two births, and my own transition into being a mother. Mom, you always offer just the right turn of phrase or insight to help me manage challenges. Where there were all the ingredients for an extended case of the baby blues, there is a book instead.

Another great fortune in my life is to have married a man who has absolute confidence in me and believes I can do anything. He might say he's my biggest fan and that is how he makes me feel. Thank you, Matt, for your encouragement as I dreamed up this book and devoted time to it over several years, for being a true partner, and for making our life as a family so much fun. If I were to step back and design my ideal life, it would be just as it is, sharing this grand adventure with you.

Without the arrival of my daughter Julia in 2002, it is fair to say there would be no book, certainly not this book, and I am thankful for her inspiration. Julia and all that she brought to my life compelled me to write this book and her brother, who arrived more recently, spurred me to extensively edit it. Were it not for baby Charles, the sleep chapter in particular would have been almost glib. Julia and Charles, the two of you fill my life with joy. I loved your little baby selves and I love getting to know you better each day for the people you are. Being your mom is the greatest pleasure of my life.

Part I
Before Baby's Arrival

Ch. 1

Chapter 1:
Preparing the Nest

At some point during your pregnancy, the moment comes when you need to set about creating a space for the newest member of your family. He or she will also require supplies, so a little shopping will be in order. This section will offer some tips and suggestions for preparing a nursery and getting a shopping list together.

As you get going, keep in mind that a "nursery" is whatever you want it to be. Our daughter lived in a walk-in closet (with a window, mind you) for the first seven months of her life. And we even decorated it: pastel sponge paints, lighting on a dimmer, and a cutesy window treatment. To a large extent, the space you have available dictates the kind of room you create and you ultimately purchase what your budget allows. Rest assured that you can design a safe, comfortable space for your baby on almost any budget.

It's easy to become overwhelmed when decorating a nursery and researching infant products. While these are really important tasks, don't lose sight of the fact that babies are generally happy if they are warm, dry, fed, and loved. The reason I mention this is that you just might find yourself in some major baby retailer eight months pregnant—ankles swelling, bladder straining—deliberating about which baby soap is the right soap for baby's tender skin. If you find yourself in this state of mind, remember that Rome was not built in a day. You do not have to purchase in advance every item you'll need until your child goes to college. You will still be able to shop after the baby is born, or at the very least send someone to the drugstore for a milder soap. It may be more practical, especially in terms of stocking medicine cabinets and the like, to plan for what you may need in the first six to eight weeks. Do your homework by talking with other moms and reading product reviews, make your lists, and above all, remain calm as you enter the ever-expanding universe of baby retail goods.

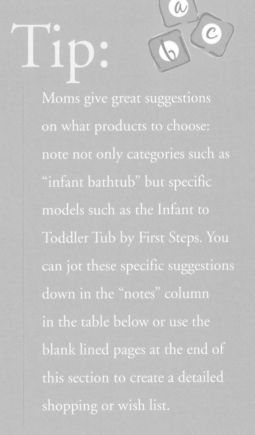

Tip:

Moms give great suggestions on what products to choose: note not only categories such as "infant bathtub" but specific models such as the Infant to Toddler Tub by First Steps. You can jot these specific suggestions down in the "notes" column in the table below or use the blank lined pages at the end of this section to create a detailed shopping or wish list.

The Goods

Shopping Lists and Suggestions

The following is a list of suggested nursery furnishings and supplies: it is not comprehensive and is intended for birth to three months. Your plans for your baby will dictate what you actually need, so use this list to help create your own shopping list. Because safety is a major concern when it comes to babies' rooms, there are some safety guidelines tucked into this checklist. Price ranges are provided for items over $50. Use the Notes section to record any brands you especially like or upcoming store sales, etc.

Ch. 1

Sleeping

Item	Description and Tips	Price range	Notes
Crib	Crib Safety standards are stringent and have been updated enormously since 1997. If you want to be positive that your crib meets current safety standards, do not buy second-hand or borrow an older crib. An easy-to-spot safety guideline: crib slats should be no more than 2⅜ inches apart and cribs currently being manufactured comply with this standard.	$200-$600	
Crib Mattress	Make sure it fits snugly in the crib. The mattress should be no more than two fingers width away from the sides of the crib.		
Crib Mattress Pad	You will need a mattress cover with a waterproof backing. Buy at least two so you can change them often.	$100-$150	

Item	Description and Tips	Price range	Notes
Crib Sheets	Two-three minimum because they need to be washed often.		
Crib Bumper/Quilt	Bumpers, which are not essential though widely used, are often sold in sets with a quilt. Quilt will be solely decorative until baby is much older.		
Bassinet	A bassinet allows your baby to room in with you for the first few months. Some parents find nighttime feedings are easier if a baby is at arm's reach. Options abound: the Moses basket is small and portable, the Pack and Play with bassinet folds up and is an essential for travel later on, the co-sleeper, which functions like a side-car, attaches to your bed, and a whole host of other choices are out there, from the frilly to the functional.	$100-$200	
Bed rail for co-sleeping	A barrier or guard rail is essential if you plan to have your baby sleep in your bed with you. It is advised that you put your baby between an adult and one side of the bed, not between two sleeping adults.		
Sleep Positioner	Designed to help prevent SIDS and keep babies snuggled in a small space in a large crib.		

Ch.
1

Feeding

An "N" indicates an item specifically for nursing mothers

Item	Description and Tips	Price range	Notes
Rocker, Glider	You will need a comfortable place to feed your baby. If you have the budget and the space, consider buying a chair for the nursery. Moms suggest buying a chair you envision in your living room in the future—multi-use makes the price easier to swallow. Another option is to look for a used chair and simply buy new cushions, usually sold separately.	$200-$600	
Nursing stool	An option much less costly than an ottoman. Nursing stools make long feeding sessions more comfortable by removing pressure on your back.		
Feeding pillow	Pillows such as the Boppy or My Brest Friend make feedings more comfortable and assist with proper positioning. Feeding pillows are also great support for an older baby learning to sit up. If you seat a baby inside the pillow, the arc shape prevents baby from falling backwards.		
Breast pump (N) (Medela double electric breast pump)	Many nursing moms find an electric breast pump essential. You can rent one to try before you decide to buy as they are costly. If you're planning to return to work and express milk, this is a must. Manual pumps exist as well.	about $250	
Formula	Ask your pediatrician to recommend a formula. Buying powdered formula, as opposed to pre-mixed, is the least expensive way to go.		

Item	Description	Price	Notes
Milk storage bags or bottles (N)	You can store and freeze breast milk for up to three months. Bags come with stickers for writing in the date. If you plan to pump and use milk in the short-term, consider milk storage bottles. Some allow you to pump and then simply screw on a nipple, converting your storage vessel into a bottle baby can drink from. This way no milk is in transfer from one container to another. Ask your pediatrician for a list of milk storage safety guidelines. Your baby will require more milk as he gains weight and your doctor will also be able to provide a chart showing the number of recommended ounces of milk in 24 hours for babies at each stage of growth.		
Bottles	Buy 2-3 if you're primarily breast-feeding and 8-10 if you plan to bottle feed exclusively. The 4 oz. size will suffice initially. You might want to start with a few different brands to see which works best for your baby (the goal is minimal air ingestion). You will also need the accompanying nipples, collars and caps.		
Dishwasher basket	Convenient way to wash nipples in the dishwasher. Later will be useful for washing teething toys and tiny utensils.		
Bottle brush	Buy one of these to clean bottles and nipples if you do not have a dishwasher.		
Bottle drying rack	Sits on the counter near the sink, allows bottles and nipples to dry in an orderly fashion.		

Ch.
1

Diapering

"D" indicates an item specifically for disposable diapers
"C" indicates an item specifically for cloth diapers

Item	Description and Tips	Price range	Notes
Changing Table	Preferably with shelving underneath and/or a drawer for storage. Alternatively, you can simply place a changing pad—a plastic contoured cushion—on a bureau top. Some moms prefer using a bureau for two reasons: the items on changing table shelves are an easy target for curious, crawling babies and re-organizing everything is tedious. Secondly, changing tables become obsolete by age 2 or so whereas a bureau is a long-term piece of furniture.	$100-$300	
Changing pad	For use with a changing table or on top of a bureau.		
Changing pad covers	Soft terrycloth covers for the changing pad. Buy 2, minimum.		
Disposable Diapers (D)	Try to have a week's supply on hand initially and buy in bulk once you assess the size of your little one. You can expect a baby to go through 10 to 12 diapers per day.		
Diaper pail (D)	Such as the Diaper Genie or Diaper Champ. Models like the Genie require special replacement canisters while the Champ allows you to use a garbage bag. These pails are designed to seal in diaper odors.		
Cloth Diapers (C)	A diaper service will deliver and pick up weekly.		
Diaper Bag or Bin (C)	Diaper service will provide at an additional cost.		

Item	Description and Tips	Price range	Notes
Diaper covers or waterproof pants (C)	Cloth diapers require a cover to be water-tight. If you use diaper covers, they fasten with velcro. (Try Bummis). If you use waterproof pants, you'll also need diaper clips to secure them.		
Wipes	For a newborn, buy unscented wipes. Have plenty on hand: 100-150 for the first week.		
Diaper cream	For diaper rash. Desitin, Triple Paste, etc. Some moms keep a tub of Vaseline handy too to help circumcisions heal.		

Outfitting

Clothing, Accessories and Toiletries

Item	Description and Tips	Price range	Notes
Onesies	The indispensable bodysuit. It is an extra layer, a T-shirt that cannot ride up, and it keeps a full diaper in check. Buy 8 minimum.		
Sleeper suits and "gowns"	PJs with feet are essential and will be worn both day and night initially. Buy about 4-5 sleepers. A nice alternative for boys and girls is the baby gown. There is elastic at the bottom but the open design allows for easy diaper changes.		

Ch. 1

Ch. 1

Item	Description and Tips	Price range	Notes
Sleep sacks	If you live in a colder climate you may want to buy a sleep sack. Sleep sacks safely envelope babies, adding an extra layer of warmth without the safety hazard of a blanket.		
"Daytime" wear	For your first outings you might like to have a few pull-on pants with elastic waist and cotton cardigans. Perhaps 3 or 4 sets.		
Socks (or booties)	6-12 pair should hold you for a while. They get swallowed in the wash easily, though!		
Hats	Babies need help to stay warm and hats are key. They're good for both outdoor and indoor wear, including during the occasional nap. Consider thin cotton caps for indoor wear. Buy 2-3.		
Receiving blankets	If you don't receive several as gifts, purchase 3-4. Great for staying warm, playtime on the floor and swaddling. You can also find blankets especially for swaddling that make a neat and tidy burrito out of your baby. Try "SwaddleMe."		
Burp-cloths	You won't know how much you'll use these until your baby arrives. Some babies spit up often, and boys tend to pee freely when exposed on the changing table. In short, a thousand uses. Buy about 12.		
Pacifiers	Buy 2 or 3 at first. Consider trying different brands to see what your baby takes to.		
Hairbrush or comb	Some babies have hair, some don't. You will eventually need this grooming accessory.		
Nail clippers	Every parent develops his or her own method for trimming nails. Eventually, you will want to have baby nail scissors or clippers on hand.		

Item	Description and Tips	Price range	Notes
Nasal Aspirator	Babies develop stuffy noses at times and need help clearing the passages. If you don't leave the hospital with this parting gift, buy one from the drugstore.		
Thermometer	The most reliable temperature readings for infants are taken rectally. Alternatively, you can buy thermometers that measure temperature in the ear. The least invasive method (and also the least accurate) is to place an oral thermometer under a baby's arm.		

Ch.
1

Tips:

Select clothes that are machine washable and that are very soft, such as jersey cotton. Consider buying sleepers that zip instead of snapping, for easier and faster changes.

Try to buy clothes in the 3-6 month window because the 0-3 month stage lasts for about 2 minutes. Plus, many people will give you teensy newborn gifts, so you'll have plenty of the little garments. Shoot for the higher sizes. Bigger is always better!

Bathing

Item	Description and Tips	Price range	Notes
Infant bathtub	Allows a baby to recline in a safe, supported position. Makes bathing more comfortable for mom and dad too (babies are slippery when wet and not always thrilled to take baths . . .)		
Hooded towels	Babies do fine with regular towels, of course, but the hooded variety are really too cute to pass up. Plus they are large enough to swaddle the freshly washed babe and keep wet heads warm. Buy 2.		
Washcloths	Tend to be smaller and lighter-weight fabric than the grown-up variety. Perfect for bathing and later, for scrubbing tiny teeth. Buy 5-10.		
Baby Shampoo/Wash	There are many nice 2-in-1 varieties or you can buy shampoo and baby wash. For the first 2-3 weeks babies are washed only with water.		

Getting Around

Item	Description and Tips	Price range	Notes
Car Seat	For infants, there are two options: an infant car seat—also known as the bucket seat—for babies up to 20 lbs. or a convertible car seat that can accommodate a baby weighing between 20-40 lbs. Many parents prefer the infant car seat because it is easily removed and carried (they have handles) so a sleeping baby can be transferred undisturbed.	$100-$300	
Diaper Bag	The backpack version keeps your hands free, the "purse-like" styles usually have pockets and compartments galore. Make sure you also have a changing pad. Tip: carry plenty of plastic bags for the dirty diapers and soiled clothes.		
Stroller	There is a world of options with strollers and this decision is, for many parents, one of the toughest. It's an expensive item, ideally you want it to take you from birth to age 2 or so, and it is not always clear before your baby arrives exactly how you will use it day to day. Some strollers are more rugged than others, some more compact. They all have pluses and minuses. At first you'll either need a fully reclining stroller or one that is compatible with an infant car seat. The latter serves the older baby as well, and hopefully saves you a second purchase. Big variety of styles, big price range.	$50-$1,000	
Baby sling or soft carrier	Some babies love being curled up in a sling for their first few months. The Baby Bjorn is also a popular baby carrier. Keeps baby snug and warm, your hands free.	$40-$100	

Ch. 1

Tip:

If you live in a colder climate and will need to transfer your baby from car to house in a car seat, consider a car seat bundler like the "Bundle Me." These are essentially sleep sacks but they have open slats to accommodate car seat straps.

Item	Description and Tips	Price range	Notes
"Snap and Go"	Consider buying/borrowing a "snap and go" frame if your lifestyle involves frequent use of a car. An infant car seat snaps into the frame and you have an instant strolling device. Also called a Universal Car Seat Carrier.	$50-$70	
Pack and Play (portable crib)	You may have purchased one of these as a bassinet. If not, you may need one when you sleep away from home. Don't forget to buy two portable crib sheets too.	$60-$200	

Play Gear and Toys

Item	Description and Tips	Price range	Notes
Bouncy Seat	Allows parents the occasional meal or shower. Bounces when baby kicks. Varying degrees of bells and whistles, buzzers and lights. Some babies like the vibration feature.	$25-$100	
Gym/Playmat	An activity mat like the popular Gymini. Baby can look at and eventually grasp toys dangling from arches overhead. Most babies really enjoy this activity.	$40-$70	
Swing	Borrow one if you can because babies either like them or they don't. Consider buying a swing that not only rocks back and forth but also side to side. Some babies prefer the lateral motion.	$70-$130	
Plush toys, Rattles, Board Books	You will most likely receive these as gifts but there may be stuffed animals, rattles, or books so cute you cannot resist. Safety dictates that any plush toy you plan to allow in the crib should not have removable parts or pieces (like buttons, for example). Toys with embroidered eyes, nose, mouth are ideal.		

Miscellaneous Items

Item	Description and Tips	Price range	Notes
Monitor	Allows you to hear your baby in other parts of the house. Buy a monitor with a visual light display as well so you will be alerted even if you're playing music, doing dishes, etc.	$25-$200	
Smoke/Carbon Monoxide Detector	These come separately or as one unit. Important safety measure for baby's room.	$40-$70	
Laundry Hamper/Basket	Keep one in baby's room if possible.		
Laundry Detergent	Babies have sensitive skin. Ideally you should wash their clothes in a mild detergent like Ivory Snow or Dreft, for the first few weeks. After that, some parents like to give regular detergent a try because separating laundry and doing several washes is not always practical. Each baby is different so you'll need to discover if your little one needs a mild detergent or can tolerate the family detergent.		
Lighting	If you can install a dimmer switch in your baby's room, it makes for less intrusive midnight encounters. An inexpensive and easy option for nighttime changes is a night light near your changing area. A lamp that sits on a bureau top is a nice alternative to an overhead light.		
Window Treatments	Window décor doesn't need to be fancy but you will want shades or curtains to block light in your baby's room.		

Parent Tips for Nursery Set-up

- Do not position a crib near a window or too close to other furniture. Older babies can use the nearby furniture and shades or blinds to assist with efforts to climb out of the crib.

- Consider positioning the bureau near the changing table. It helps to be able to reach a clean set of clothes while keeping one hand on your baby.

- If you are going to use crib bumpers, once your baby starts moving around, consider tying the bumpers on the outside of the crib. This prevents little arms and legs from getting caught between slats but does not present the same entanglement danger as bumpers on the inside of the crib.

- Childproof the nursery: install outlet covers, furniture fasteners to prevent tipping, door-knob covers if the door locks from the inside, an escape ladder if the room is above the first floor. If your drapes or blinds have cords, buy devices that allow you to roll them up so they are out of reach.

- If you hang any art in the nursery, avoid the area near the crib. If you have any art framed, choose Plexiglas because it does not shatter when it breaks.

- If you have a thick carpet in the nursery, consider buying a glider instead of a rocker. Gliders are a smooth ride no matter what the surface.

- If your nursery is not carpeted, consider buying a plush area rug that will become a play space.

- If you have space and the budget, consider buying a small bookcase for the nursery. You will soon need a place to store baby's growing library.

- Toy storage: your baby will collect toys quickly and you may need a storage solution. If you buy a toy bin with a lid of any kind, make sure that there is space for air to penetrate if a child were to become trapped inside the toy chest. Many toy bins do not have lids for safety reasons.

Resources:

Product reviews and finding the deals

Books:

• *Baby Bargains: Secrets to Saving 20% to 50% on Baby Furniture, Equipment, Clothes, Toys, Maternity Wear, and Much, Much More!* by Denise Fields

• *The Girlfriends' Guide to Baby Gear: What to Buy, What to Borrow, and What to Blow Off* by Vicky Iovine and Peg Rosen

• *Baby Stuff: A No-Nonsense Shopping Guide for Every Parent's Lifestyle* by Ari Lipper and Joanna Lipper

• *Nighttime Parenting* by Dr. William Sears

For co-sleeping safety guidelines and suggested gear

Books:

• *Good Nights: The Happy Parents' Guide to the Family Bed (And a Peaceful Night's Sleep,*
Practical suggestions for accomplishing a family bed arrangement.

Online:

• http://store.babycenter.com/checklists

• www.1800diapers.com
Great deals on disposable diapers, wipes, and formula, shipped right to your door.

Safety and Childproofing

Books:

• *On the Safe Side: Your Complete Reference to Childproofing for Infants and Toddlers,* by Cindy Wolf

Online:

• www.cpsc.gov
US Consumer Product Safety Commission

• www.recalls.gov
Extremely user-friendly site, search for recalls by category

• www.jpma.org
Juvenile Products Manufacturing Association

my list . . . _____

_____

_____

_____

_____

_____

_____

_____

_____

_____

_____

_____

Ch. 1

**Ch.
1**

Borrowed Items

This space is to record anything you're able to borrow. This is especially useful if you borrow—or lend—maternity clothes because it's hard to keep track of every little item. You may want to write in the owner's phone or email as well.

Item	Owner	Returned
		☐
		☐
		☐
		☐
		☐
		☐
		☐
		☐
		☐
		☐
		☐
		☐
		☐
		☐

Ch. 1

Item	Owner	Returned
		☐
		☐
		☐
		☐
		☐
		☐
		☐
		☐
		☐
		☐
		☐
		☐
		☐
		☐
		☐
		☐
		☐
		☐

Naming Baby

There are only a few questions people ask when you announce you're pregnant: "When are you due?" "Do you know what you're having?" and "Have you chosen a name?" Naming your baby is one of the joys of being pregnant and imagining the little someone who is on the way. It's fun to daydream about names, joke about them, and throw ideas around for months before this person enters the world. Naming a baby is also one of your many responsibilities as a future parent. Names are pretty permanent, after all.

Family and friends—and perfect strangers—tend to have a lot of opinions about names. A name can mean so much to every member of the family. You can decide how many people you want to consult and whether or not you'll keep your cards close to your vest until the baby arrives. It can be difficult to hear suggestions from family and then choose another name entirely.

Ultimately, you're in charge this time around and you can name your baby anything that is meaningful to you.

Of course, there is one person that you will need to not only consult, but agree with about the baby's name. Your spouse has a list too. Combine lists, make a shorter list from your longer lists, discuss (there may be more than one discussion involved, be forewarned) and by the big day, it's a safe bet that you will have arrived at that special combination of letters that will be immeasurably important to you and your baby.

Chances are that you already have some favorite names in mind. Over the years we all make a mental note of names that strike us, even if naming our firstborn is not imminent. You know the names that you would never choose in a million years (that nemesis from the third grade who you can never forget) and you can effortlessly rule out names that rhyme with your last name,

Ch. 1

names of ex-boyfriends, and names that, when combined, form the name of a well-known location, celebrity or a major corporation. There is currently a major league baseball player named Milton Bradley, celebrity and corporation at once.

You may want to buy or borrow a book on names. It can be fun to peruse the pages late

What's in a Name?

Here are some factors to consider when selecting names:

Spelling: Most names have a traditional spelling but that doesn't mean you can't vary it. For example, you may prefer Merry to Mary. If you consider an unusual spelling, ask yourself if it will make your child feel unique or if it will be annoying to have to spell out his/her name all the time. Put yourself in your child's shoes and it will become clear whether an alternate spelling is an asset or an albatross.

Initials: You might not have mono-grammed towels in your bathroom but it's worth thinking about what your baby's initials will spell. Don't give the playground thugs an edge.

Meaning: Most names have an origin (nationality) and a meaning. If you love a name but don't especially like its meaning, that does not rule it out. Most people only know the meaning of their own name or those in their family. This universe of name meanings is highly subjective, so you can decide how important it is for you.

Syllables/rhythm: Some naming gurus suggest that names with a varying num-ber of syllables have a nice sound when paired. In other words, if your last name has one syllable, consider a first name with two. For example, Hannah Smith

into the night, become delirious from looking at so many, and laugh the next day because the name you felt so sure about now looks outrageous in the light of day. Often, these lists and the meanings and origins of names help you think of ideas that would not occur to you otherwise. See the Resources section for a list of baby name books.

sounds different than Ann Smith. Again, subjective, but useful to consider.

Popularity: There are two sides to the coin here: the popularity you seek and the popularity you seek to avoid. It would be naïve to claim that names don't immediately conjure associations and stereotypes. You may want to choose a name that is popular in the sense that it has positive associations for most people. Depending on your heritage or background, this can include a wide range of names but these are names that might connote power, optimism, strength, perhaps femininity, and other valued qualities.

The other popularity is the kind you may want to avoid, which is when your son meets six other Jacobs in his preschool class. For some parents it's important that a name be unique in all the world and others don't mind at all if their child has classmates of the same name.

Trends now: Traditional names are making a comeback. Names that were popular at the turn of the century—the previous century—such as Thomas and Abigail, are rising in the ranks, giving the Madisons and Aidans a run for their money. Name ranking can be useful as you make a decision and you can find this information online easily. See the Resources section for suggestions.

Ch. 1

So, have some fun. Make yourself a long list.

Daydream about that future concert pianist, that wrestling champion, that...

Girls Names	Boys Names	Middle Names/Notes
_____	_____	_____
_____	_____	_____
_____	_____	_____
_____	_____	_____
_____	_____	_____
_____	_____	_____
_____	_____	_____
_____	_____	_____

Check out these books:

The Baby Name Wizard: A Magical Method for Finding the Perfect Name for Your Baby by Laura Wallenberg

Beyond Jennifer and Jason, Madison & Montana: What to Name Your Baby Now by Linda Rosenkrantz

Best Baby Name Book in the Whole World by Bruce Lansky

Como Te Llamas, Baby?: The Hispanic Baby Name Book by Jamie Martinez Wood and Catherine Martinez

Or these websites:

Social Security Online:
www.ssa.gov/OACT/babynames/

www.babycenter.com/pregnancy/baby naming/index

Have a Baby, Get an Education

The propagation of humankind over centuries has proven that no actual training is required to birth and nurture a newborn. However, we highly evolved beings find ways to prepare when we can. And although the only real way to learn about caring for your baby is to do it, many new parents like to get ready for this experience by taking classes related to childbirth and parenting a newborn. Even if a class cannot prepare you for every scenario, gathering information in advance can boost your confidence.

You'll have to see what's available in your community and decide which classes will be of most use given your circumstances. Most hospitals with maternity services offer pregnancy and parenting classes and you may find additional offerings at a local resource center for parents.

The list below describes some classes that may interest you. If you find one of the topics especially relevant and cannot find a class in your area, at least you can do some reading on the topic and access online resources prior to your baby's arrival.

Ch. 1

Before Your Baby Arrives

Most of these classes are taken in the second or third trimesters of pregnancy. You may want to register early to get the sessions that fit your schedule.

Breast-feeding Usually taught by a certified lactation consultant, this class covers the benefits and basic techniques of breast-feeding. The class may include topics such as establishing a milk supply, let-down, latch-on, correct positioning, choosing a breast pump, and milk storage. Most breast-feeding classes also discuss how to overcome challenges as you begin breast-feeding and manage any difficulties that may arise.

Ch. 1

Breast-feeding Multiples A lactation consultant discusses special considerations for breast-feeding twins and triplets.

Childbirth Preparation The focus of these classes varies a great deal but most provide an overview of the stages and process of labor and talk about a variety of breathing and relaxation techniques to reduce discomfort during labor. You'll also learn about medicated pain relief options during labor and possible medical procedures, including cesarean birth. Most classes include a discussion about the immediate postpartum care of mother and baby.

Childbirth Preparation: Birth Alternatives If you're interested in a natural birth experience, you may be able to find a class with an emphasis on labor support techniques. While you may not find this class at your hospital, there are usually options in the wider community. You can search for classes based on a specific birth method,

such as Bradley, or seek an integrated approach. Your doctor or midwife might have some good suggestions on where to start your search.

Newborn Parenting This class offers tips on surviving the first few weeks with your baby. Topics usually include diapering, bathing, swaddling, and soothing techniques as well as newborn appearance and behavior. Many parents find that this type of class eases their transition when returning home from the hospital.

Infant/Child CPR This covers vital skills to handle an emergency: how to recognize an infant or child in distress, perform emergency measures to relieve airway obstruction in a choking infant or child, perform CPR on an infant or child who is not

Ch. 1

breathing, and identify preventable child-hood injuries. Many parents find this class essential and request that family members and childcare providers take it, too.

First Aid This usually covers basic first aid, safety precautions, stocking your first aid box and medicine cabinet, and how to handle childhood accidents. Sometimes these topics are included in an infant/child CPR class.

Expecting Twins or More This class gives parents advice and discusses practical considerations about raising twins. Topics can include prenatal care, labor and delivery, feeding, and preparing your home and family for the arrival of your babies.

Choosing Childcare Discusses childcare options and strategies for finding a solution to fit your lifestyle. Not widely offered: you may need to consult books, friends, and other resources.

After Your Baby Is Born

Breast-feeding and Working This class provides practical tips on continuing to breastfeed your baby while working. Topics include: preserving the breast-feeding relationship, choosing a breastpump, collecting, storing and transporting breastmilk, introducing the bottle, maintaining your milk supply, combining breast-feeding with formula feeding, and exploring child-care options.

Baby Massage These classes teach a progression of simple techniques and strokes that promote relaxation in you and your infant. Techniques for relieving colic are often covered. The instructor will help you discover creative ways to incorporate massage into your lives, often through games and songs.

Baby Signs This class helps you learn a basic sign language vocabulary and use signs to stimulate your baby's intelligence and decrease frustration.

Ch. 1

Notes . . . _____

_____

_____

_____

_____

_____

_____

_____

_____

_____

_____

_____

_____

_____

Selecting a Pediatrician

"...parents know they will need a pediatrician and advocate for the baby and are eager to share their hopes and concerns. They wonder who this child will be. I can uncover and share their anxieties with them. I see this as the first 'touchpoint,' an opportunity for me to make a relationship with each parent before there is a baby between us."

—T. Berry Brazelton, M.D., *Touchpoints*

Ch. 1

Taking the time to meet with two or three different pediatricians during your third trimester can be a tremendous advantage once your baby is born. In the weeks following the birth of your baby, you will most likely visit with your pediatrician and may need to check in by phone as well.

While the doctor you choose will care for your baby, it is you who will do all the communicating initially. It matters that you like the doctor's communication style and manner and that you can discuss concerns openly with him or her. Especially when there are bumps in the road, you will be reassured by contact with someone you respect and trust.

One of the best ways to find a good pediatrician is to ask friends, neighbors and others in your community what practice their child goes to and why they like a particular doctor.

When you call to schedule a meeting with a pediatrician, consider asking office staff about these topics:

● **Which insurance an office accepts. Being in- or out-of-network for your insurance carrier may make the decision for you.**

● **Consider the background and training of the doctor, especially if you prefer that he/ she speak a language other than English.**

● **Billing procedures and the financial policy of the office.**

● **Office hours**

● **Availability of an advice line and/or drop-in urgent care**

Pediatrician Interview

Before your baby is born you may want to meet a few pediatricians before choosing a practice. You can use these questions to help guide your search.

Most doctors will not charge for an interview. Expect to spend about 15 to 20 minutes with a pediatrician for a consultation.

Name: _____

Address: _____

Phone/Email: _____

1. Some questions you may want to ask:

How long have you been in practice? _____

Are you part of a group practice? _____

If it's a group practice, will we always be able to have appointments with you?

_____

What are your hours? _____

Ch.
1

Typically, how far in advance would we need to schedule a well-baby visit? A week? A month? More? (How busy is this practice? Reassuringly busy or too busy?)

_____

Does your practice offer drop-in urgent care? _____

Is there a doctor on call for evenings and weekends? _____

Are you available to answer routine non-emergency questions by phone or email?

_____

Which hospital is your practice affiliated with? _____

Do you have a particular philosophy or approach for parenting that you recommend to new parents? _____

. . . .

2. Express your views or questions on some of the following issues to see if the doctor shares your outlook or is open to your point of view:

Bottle feeding/Breast-feeding or a combination_____

Pacifiers_____

Co-sleeping_____

Sleep training/techniques_____

Ch. 1

Circumcision_____

Discipline_____

Notes:_____

_____

_____

_____

_____

_____

_____

3. Consider your general feeling about the doctor and practice:_____

_____

Did you leave the interview feeling comfortable with the doctor?_____

What did the doctor say that was reassuring or made you feel at ease?_____

Was there anything you and the doctor clearly disagreed about?_____

How long did the doctor spend with you?_____

Can you get to the office easily (without switching buses or sitting in traffic for hours)?_____

Was the office and waiting room clean?_____

Were administrative staff friendly and helpful?_____

Is this a person you would like to see and talk with if your child was unwell?

Notes:_____

_____

_____

_____

_____

_____

_____

_____

Ch.
1

Ch.
2

Chapter 2:
Preparing Yourself

During pregnancy, especially your first, there is so much to think about. You gather information about the different stages of pregnancy, you sign up for childbirth and baby care classes, you try to eat healthy food. It's easy to spend your time doting on your baby—and pregnant self—and forget to look at what's coming around the bend. At the end of this pregnancy odyssey, you don't get to rest on your laurels: you'll have a baby to care for. And that's why this is a good time to focus on logistics and concerns beyond a perfectly appointed nursery. Even that wipe warmer is not going to solve everything, although babies probably prefer warm bums.

The way to get things in order for the weeks following your baby's arrival is to line up some help, plain and simple. Even if you think you were born to be a parent and you don't need any help, you may.

Ch.
2

Everyone can use an extra pair of hands to match up 57 tiny, freshly-laundered socks and everyone can use a break to get out in the sunshine. For many women, this help is offered by a relative or close friend. Think about who you would like to have with you in the early weeks and then work out a plan. If you do turn out to be a super-being, you can always politely postpone visits from would-be helpers.

"But wait!" you object. "There are two of us and just one, small baby. What could be so hard?" Two words for you: sleep deprivation. Count on some help from someone who is getting more sleep than you are.

If you don't have a relative or friend who fits the bill, consider hiring help for a period of time. It's an expense, yes, but the women who offer these services would say it's an investment (in your own sanity). Hiring help in the form of childcare or a postpartum doula gets you and your baby off to the right start: good eating, good sleeping, good emotional health for mom. If you have those three things during the first few months your baby is in the world, you are in great shape.

Tip:

Reliable, scheduled help is often better than spotty drop-in help. It's nice to be able to count on a break at a certain time or know that your mountain of laundry will be dealt with before noon. Sometimes paying for help, even an hour or two a week, can offer a big relief.

Planning for Help at Home:

Gifts come in many shapes and sizes—and flavors. You'll find that as your due date approaches, many friends and coworkers will ask what they can do to help you. And you will appreciate the sentiment but will probably not reply "could you bring dinner over every Monday for three weeks?"

Julie Bouchet Horwitz, a lactation consultant at Nyack Hospital in New York, has found a way to harness the good-will expressed by your friends and put it into action. The Postpartum Plan™ (PPP) is essentially a chore wheel but in this case the chores are your family's postpartum needs. The idea is to get your network of friends in touch and have them divvy up tasks to lighten your load for the first few weeks postpartum. These favors can replace traditional shower gifts or be given instead of "welcome" presents for the new baby. There are times when you'll need a home-cooked dinner more than that extra receiving blanket.

The most expedient way to get your "plan" ironed out is to ask one friend to coordinate the effort. Often someone hosting a shower for you is a good choice. You can let her know what you think you'll need help with and then she can ask the friends on your list what they can do. Don't worry, your coordinator can let people know that participation is optional and that there will be no hard feelings if someone can't help out, no excuses needed.

Think of the possibilities! Imagine that you have this help for four weeks. It is minimal effort for your friends in the scheme of things and it will make your life so much easier. Here's a sample PPP based on help from six friends:

Mondays:

- Erin: dinner (cook and deliver two meals over a month)

- Beth: dinner (cook and deliver two meals over a month)

- Erin and Beth alternate every other Monday. You get fed every Monday for a month.

Tuesdays:

- Rebecca: drive Jed from school to soccer practice, 3:00. (Four rides and maybe Rebecca has a child in the same school so it's no big deal for her to pick Jed up too. Jed is your older child, by the way.)

Wednesdays:

- Aunt Lorraine: Grocery store, other errands (Aunt Lorraine is retired and has time for this)

Thursdays:

- You're on your own. Order pizza.

Fridays:

- Meagan: Brings you take-out food. (Delivery of 4 take-out meals. Meagan doesn't cook so it makes her feel really good to bring you nourishment. You pay for the food, she just brings it and sometimes even stays to eat with you—an added bonus: socializing.)

Saturdays:

- Emily: stops by in the afternoon to do some baby laundry and entertain baby so you can nap for an hour.

Sundays:

- Day of rest for all except Junior and his busy parents.

. . . .

Does it seem like too much to ask? It's a gift everyone feels good about giving. And it's a good bet your close friends and family will be happy to cook a meal or two for you. People are usually happy to help; they just need some direction in this case. And anyone who is a mom would jump at the chance to help a new mom through a wonderful, yet tiring, first month or two with a baby. This plan does not need to go into effect in week one. You can implement it after your relatives return home or whenever you'll need help most. You'll find a worksheet in this chapter that you can remove and give to your coordinator if you want to give this a try.

Ch. 2

If you like the idea of a PPP, here are some things to consider asking for help with:

- **Meals**
- **Light grocery shopping**
- **Light housekeeping**
- **Drug store, post office, other errands**
- **Care for an older child**

Professional Mother's Helpers: Doulas

"Doula" is derived from the Greek "doulos." This Greek word referred to a servant in the household who cared for new mothers. A modern-day doula is a woman who provides non-clinical physical, emotional, and informational support to a childbearing woman and her family.

Some doulas specialize in birth and assist couples during labor. A doula present at a birth can help interpret medical information and help parents make decisions during a very intense time. A doula does not offer medical advice. Doulas care for moms, suggesting new birthing positions, offering hands-on comfort when appropriate, giving reassurance, and taking care of needs. During birth a doula can offer the support care that nurses, midwives, and doctors may not be available to give because of their clinical responsibilities.

Other doulas offer postpartum support for moms and families. Postpartum doulas offer reassurance, breast-feeding support and other assistance to new mothers. Doulas also help with infant care and light housekeeping. Postpartum doulas are an emerging group that is growing as more women discover the benefits of this kind of support following birth. Historically, new mothers had other women around them, often living in multigenerational homes. Now many mothers, urban and suburban alike, feel isolated when they arrive home with a new baby. A doula can help alleviate this sense of isolation and offer the

knowledge and support that a community of women did in earlier times.

For more information about doulas and some suggestions on how to locate a doula in your area, see the interview in this chapter and the Resources section.

Maternity Leave

If you're working during your pregnancy, the time will come when you need to tell your manager and coworkers that you are expecting. In general, it's not wise to talk about your pregnancy at work during the first trimester because the risk of miscarriage is still a factor. If you wait too long, though, people will begin to see a tell-tale bump appearing and want to share in your

excitement. So somewhere between the end of the first trimester and beginning to look undeniably pregnant, you need to share your news. It's good form to let your manager know first before going public with other co-workers.

Depending on the type of work you do and the culture of your workplace, making this announcement can feel somewhat

....

When you are ready to let your manager know that you're pregnant, pick a time that's low stress for both of you. A busy Monday morning right before an important meeting is not a good time. A slower Friday afternoon when there's nothing scheduled is better. In other words, take the recipient's state of mind into account before launching into your news.

....

daunting. After all, pregnancies and babies are just never in synch with project schedules and deadlines. I dreaded breaking the news that my indispensable skills would not be available for a few months. Turns out, nobody was shocked by the baby news, and

in reality they could do without me for a little while (who knew?). I even received congratulations. Don't worry too much because nobody actually tells you that you are letting the team down and for the most part, nobody feels that way.

It's a good idea to begin investigating your company's maternity leave or family leave policy as soon as you have broadcast your happy news. When it comes to maternity leave policies, America does not measure up to other nations. The sad truth is that only about 25 percent of companies in the U.S. currently offer paid maternity or family leave as a benefit. If you work for a company that does, you're very lucky. If you don't, you may still be entitled to an unpaid leave but you may have more work to do in order to find out how the policy works and whether or not you will qualify for other paid benefits such as state disability. In many states, if your company does not offer paid leave or only offers a percentage of your regular salary, state disability will augment this.

. . . .

Don't plan to discuss your maternity or family leave with your manager in the same moment that you announce you're pregnant. There's plenty of time to talk about that, and if you have an HR department at work, that's a more appropriate place for a conversation about benefits. The best way to begin gathering information about your company's leave policy is to talk to co-workers who have had babies. They'll know the policies inside and out.

. . . .

Some states have their own FMLA policies that can extend your leave. States can offer you more than the federal policy but not less. For example, California offers an additional twelve weeks of unpaid leave. Moms and dads there can take six months off from work and be guaranteed a job when they return. Be sure to find out about your state's policies.

Regardless of your politics, we all owe President Clinton some thanks because he forever changed the course of maternity leave policy in the U.S. when he signed the Family Medical Leave Act (FMLA) into law in 1993. The FMLA applies to companies with 50 or more employees and requires your employer to allow you twelve weeks of unpaid leave each year for the birth or adoption of a child. Birth mothers, fathers,

and adoptive mothers and fathers are eligible, provided they have worked at a company for one year and worked at least 1,250 hours per year. To take advantage of this benefit, you must take your leave within twelve months of your child's birth or adoption. You will need to provide documentation of your child's birth or placement to qualify for leave under the FMLA.

FMLA was a progressive step for a few reasons: it includes fathers and adoptive parents—and for all parents this law, for the first time, ensures that your leave is job-protected. This means that when you return, you are guaranteed a job. Your employer is not required to hold your position for you but is required by law to offer you a similar position.

For biological moms and dads and adoptive parents alike, the goal is the same: to spend as much time with your infant as you can and find a way to replace as much of your paycheck as possible while you're out of work. While you are asking around at work

Ch. 2

and talking with HR, you should also contact your state Department of Labor to find out what employers in your state are legally required to offer. Once you know what kind of leave and benefits you can expect from your employer, you can research whether or not your state offers disability benefits and find out if you are eligible.

Creating a Birth Plan

As your due date approaches, no doubt your thoughts are shifting from the day-to-day survival of the third trimester to the upcoming birth of your baby. We women of the twenty-first century are fortunate in that we have a lot of choices and options around birth. When I was pregnant, I reveled in this. I wanted to create the perfect experience: ideal for me and my baby. I began to think about a plan. Maybe you've heard about birth plans and

had someone suggest you write one.

Setting out to create a birth plan requires that you gather information and form opinions about childbirth practices. This process is a way to educate yourself about birth and baby-related procedures, some standard, some not. The knowledge you gain will serve you well during your birth and after your baby is born. Creating a plan can also help open a dialog between you and your health care provider and offer a chance to discuss what is important to you. For these reasons, at least thinking about a birth plan, if not actually writing one, is often valuable.

Although birth plans can be useful and important, I personally feel they should be relabeled birth preferences. Researching options and developing birth preferences allows you to have a vision of the birth experience you want. But because birth is unpredictable, the illusion of choice can sometimes create disappointment. There are many moms who feel disappointed when their birthing experience does not go according to "plan" and is less than ideal in their eyes. Focus on the knowledge-gathering aspect of birth planning instead of the plan part and you will be better off.

If you explore every corner of the birthing universe, make an informed decision about where and how to have a baby, and then have these plans abruptly change at the last moment, a birth plan was still an essential tool. You'll be all the more prepared to deal with the unexpected because you educated yourself about birth in a variety of settings and circumstances.

There is some question as to whom a birth plan ultimately serves. Ostensibly, it's for your care-providers so that they know how you would like yourself and your baby cared for. But one could argue that a birth plan is more about self-discovery than for any external purpose. A maternity ward in most hospitals is a beehive of activity. It would be the unusual doctor or nurse who had time to read each patient's birth plan and customize the care of each mother, each child. If you have strong opinions about your care, you'll need to voice them as things come up, whether you have a birth plan or not. Don't assume that handing a written plan to your healthcare provider is going to convey all your desires. Speak up!

Below are some suggestions for thinking through birth options. This is not a complete list. You can use it as a jumping off point or use it to refine what you're already mulling over. Many of these questions don't have to be decided in advance, but you might feel better about making decisions when the time comes if you've already done some research.

My Plan

During Birth:

Where do you want to give birth?

- In a hospital? _____
- In a birth center? _____
- At home? _____

. . . .

Who would you like to care for you?

- A doctor? _____
- A midwife? _____
- Other? _____

. . . .

Who else do you envision attending your birth?

- Relative? _____
- Friend? _____
- Doula? _____

. . . .

What do you hope the setting will be like during labor?

- Much support from nurses and doctors? _____

- Bustling activity (visits from friends or family)? _____
- Quiet and private? _____
- Other? _____

. . . .

What technique or strategy have you thought about for managing pain in labor?

- Pain medication? _____
- Breathing or relaxation technique such as Lamaze or Bradley Method? _____
- Bath or shower? _____
- Other? _____

. . . .

Are there any special birthing customs in your culture that you plan to draw on?

_____

_____

_____

_____

After Baby Is Born:

How do you plan to feed your baby?

- Breast-feed? _____

- Formula? _____

- Combination? _____

· · · · · · · · · · · ·

Where would you prefer that your baby sleep?

- In the nursery? _____

- In your room (assuming the hospital allows this)? _____

- A little of each? _____

· · · · · · · · · · · ·

Other baby care options during a hospital stay:

- Pacifier use: if you don't want your baby to have one in the nursery, say so. _____

- Breast-feeding: on-demand or on a schedule? _____

- Circumcision (boys): yes or no. If yes, during hospital stay?

  _____

- Tests: if you wish to accompany your baby to the nursery for routine tests, make this known.

· · · · · · · · · · · ·

Resources:

Doulas:

Doulas of North America: www.dona.org

Association of Labor Assistants and Childbirth Educators: www.alace.org

Maternity/Family Leave:

For a list of state labor offices: www.dol.gov/esa/contacts/state_of.htm

For information about the Family Medical Leave Act: www.dol.gov/esa/whd/fmla/index.htm

Birth Plans:

Baby Center offers a comprehensive resource for creating a birth plan. This site provides an interactive worksheet and includes an incredible array of options. Many of the topics have links to help you with further research as well. http://www.babycenter.com/calculators/birthplan/

Ch. 2

Birth Preferences

You can complete this worksheet and give it to your doctor or hospital staff

Mom and Dad: _____

Doctor: _____

Other attendant (Doula, midwife, relative): _____

Allergies to Medication: _____

During the birth of our baby:

1. _____

2. _____

3. _____

4. _____

5. _____

After our baby is born:

1. _____

2. _____

3. _____

4. _____

5. _____

Thank you for taking the time to read about and consider our preferences.

The Postpartum Plan™
Coordinator Worksheet

To the Mother:

1. Fill in the names, phone numbers and e-mail addresses of friends, neighbors, co-workers and relatives whom you think would be interested in participating in your postpartum care. Try to put the names of the people closest to you at the top.

2. Indicate the category of help you think would be most appropriate for them.

   Categories: M = Meals   H = Housekeeping

   E = Errands   C = Childcare

3. List any food restrictions you may have.

4. Give this list and two or three blank copies of the calendar to a close friend or relative who can serve as the coordinator.

- -

To the Coordinator:

1. Call each person on the list after the baby is born. Inform her that you are organizing a postpartum care plan as a present for the mother and that you are hoping she can participate.

   Ask her what she would like to help with (meals, errands, housekeeping, or child-care), letting her know that it's okay to decline.

2. Write each participant's name on the calendar, indicate what she will help with using the letter codes below, and fill in the date(s) assigned.

3. Give the mother the filled-in calendar.

Ch. 2

1. _____

2. _____

3. _____

4. _____

5. _____

6. _____

7. _____

8. _____

9. _____

10. _____

11. _____

12. _____

Food Restrictions _____

_____

_____

month: .... helper: ....

sun	mon	tues	wed	thurs	fri	sat

The Postpartum Plan™ Calendar   Julie Bouchet Horwitz FNP, IBCLC ©1995

notes: _____

_____

_____

Ch.
2

month: ....   helper: ....

sun	mon	tues	wed	thurs	fri	sat

The Postpartum Plan™ Calendar   Julie Bouchet Horwitz FNP, IBCLC ©1995

notes: _____

_____

_____

month: ....   helper: ....

sun	mon	tues	wed	thurs	fri	sat

The Postpartum Plan™ Calendar   Julie Bouchet Horwitz FNP, IBCLC ©1995

notes: _____

_____

_____

Objectives for an Interview with a Birth or Postpartum Doula

Plan to talk with a few doulas by phone and then set up meetings with those you feel may be a good match. In addition to information-gathering, don't forget to rely on your instincts: if you feel like a particular doula will be a great support person for you, she probably will. Use the space below to make notes from your conversations and record contact information.

When talking with a doula, you will want to find out:

- **Is the doula DONA* certified or pursuing certification? *Stands for Doulas of North America but the organization is now known as DONA, International.**

- **In addition to any certification, what other field(s) has she worked in?**

- **How does the doula view her role? What will she help with, and how?**

- **Does she have a particular philosophy about labor, birth or the care of newborns?**

- **How will she balance caring for me and also helping care for my baby? How will she prioritize? (Postpartum doula)**

- **Does she have experience working in particular hospitals or other birth settings?**

- **Does she have relationships with doctors, nurses, midwives or lactation consultants at local hospitals or in the community?**

- **Does she have knowledge of other community resources?**

- **Ask for two or three references, from families that she has worked with before. Follow up by contacting them.**

- _____

- _____

- _____

Ask an Expert

Interview with Margaret Bergmann-Ness, Postpartum Doula and Psychotherapist

What is the role of a postpartum doula?

Essentially, it is to care for parents so that they have more energy and capacity to learn about their babies. The goal is to always be in service of the mother and other parent. When the mother has adequate physical, educational, and emotional support, she will more quickly and smoothly be able to care for and bond with her baby.

And what kind of tasks are in a postpartum doula's job description?

Well, a wide range of tasks, from meal preparation and household organization, and education about normal newborn behaviors, to emotional support. For example, one important part of this work is sitting with mom during feedings, whether breast- or bottle-feeding, and helping her figure out what's going on. If feeding is going smoothly, a doula can offer education and reassurance about cues that the feeding is going well—for example, that the baby looks content, that mother can hear swallowing sounds—or figure out ways to adjust pillows to support the baby. If things are not going so well, a doula can offer suggestions to help with typical problems and refer to a lactation specialist when appropriate.

Another important task is that doulas listen. Part of the role is validating the chaos of the postpartum period. To let moms know that it's appropriate to feel topsy-turvy, vulnerable, and raw. To help moms understand that getting outside your normal, adult way of functioning and being more emotionally chaotic is a way of getting to know your baby. If you remained in your usual adult state of mind, it would not be the same kind of bonding process.

**Ch.
2**

That's such an important message to new moms, that the rocky emotions actually open you up and allow you to connect with your new baby.

Yes, and at the same time, another part of the role is to make order out of chaos in the physical environment. You want a doula who can walk in and see what needs to be done, prioritize. Experience helps you to know when care for mom, such as listening and feeding support, needs to come before cleaning dishes or housekeeping.

Doulas should have good information about normal baby development and behavior. This is important because a large part of what doulas do is reassure about what's normal.

In addition, doulas need to know when to refer a mom to a specialist. When to stop reassuring and say, let's call your OB-Gyn or your pediatrician. A doula should have good knowledge of community resources such as support groups for new moms, counseling and therapy practices, and play groups.

When does a postpartum doula appear on the scene?

Typically, a couple meets with a doula during pregnancy to develop a rough plan. It is important to hook up very soon after birth. Many doulas come to the family's home within a day or so of the birth, some may visit at the hospital before the family goes home.

How long do parents typically work with a postpartum doula?

Depending on the circumstances, a typical time frame might be one or two months. Often a doula comes to the house a few times a week for a few hours each visit. It is important to have this consistency so that the family can count on the assistance and so that the doula can build up trust and familiarity with the family. Often, people will taper off on the frequency and length of their visits after the first few weeks. And of course different families and different doulas work within a wide range of schedules. Some doulas contract for a minimum number of hours. Some new families, especially if they are having twins or triplets, hire doulas to help by staying over the whole night, maybe a few times a week. Some new families want just a few hours here and there during the first week.

What can a doula offer a family in the postpartum period that a family member cannot?

Of course, this depends on specific family dynamics. There are a few ways a doula can be of help that are often harder for family members: an important part of a doula's job is listening and exchanging ideas with the new mother. The doula's professional role adds a bit of distance, or objectivity, so that a doula can hear what a mom is saying as being about the mom. Also, a doula can listen without moving quickly into giving advice and trying to "fix" things, instead helping the parents to gradually discover their own solutions.

Also, things have changed with baby care. In many cases, today's grandmothers did not breast-feed their children. If a mom wants to breast-feed, it is important to have someone present who is trained in breast-feeding support. A doula will help a mom and baby establish breast-feeding and reassure mom that the baby is fine, the baby is not hungry, that the milk will come in. Or she can refer to a specialist when things are difficult. In the first few days and weeks of breast-feeding, it's helpful to have someone to check in with when you have doubts.

I think that given the option, many new moms would like to have the support of a postpartum doula. How costly is it to hire a doula?

It is an investment, but I also think it is a good time to invest for many reasons. Postpartum doulas usually charge $25 to $35 per hour. Newly trained doulas will sometimes be able to work for reduced fees to gain experience and references.

What are the reasons you think this is a good time to invest?

First, if everything gets off to a smooth start, the whole family is better off.

Physically, women can recover more quickly if they have enough help after birth, instead of getting deeply in debt with fatigue by feeling pressure to get back on top of everything right away. Emotionally, mothers and fathers can give more to their infant if they get enough support at this time. On a strictly financial level, if breast-feeding succeeds, a family saves a lot of money on formula costs in the first year.

Also, this professional contract buys a family security. Often, family members and friends want to help but cannot commit to a predictable schedule. A family who hires a doula can count on help at predictable times, a very valuable thing during a chaotic period of life.

What if you don't seek out a postpartum doula prior to the birth of your baby but then decide a week or two in that you need some support?

You can contact a doula any time! They will never tell you it's too late. There are people who prearrange to work with doulas and those who discover they need help after birth. The doula network is very responsive, so even though a particular doula may not be able to help you right away, she will help you find someone who can.

What is the best way to find a doula?

It depends on where you live. In some areas, doulas advertise and it's easy to find people. A great resource is DONA, International (formerly called DONA, for Doulas of North America). Using their website, dona.org, you can find a certified doula for labor or postpartum or you can find DONA members who are working toward certification.

Certification for postpartum doulas is fairly new, so there are many more certified birth doulas than postpartum doulas.

Why is that?

Maybe because birth is so exciting and postpartum care is not seen as quite as *thrilling. Also, there is a social expectation in our country that moms should be able to handle everything on their own. We are just starting to consider the benefits of support for new mothers following the birth of a baby.*

Do many doulas work with couples for both labor and postpartum?

It is hard to say. Many birth doulas do some support postpartum without calling themselves postpartum doulas. I could guess that maybe 50 percent of doulas do both things? But I'm sure there is a lot of variation from one region of the country to another. Many couples have a doula for either labor or postpartum.

Many postpartum doulas do not assist with births because there is the risk of a conflict: it's hard to offer consistent postpartum support to a mother if you're on call for births. A postpartum doula is there to offer predictable support; if you're doing both it is very hard to manage it seamlessly.

Do you have any other words of advice for new moms?

Postpartum doulas can be great listeners and supporters, but there is a tendency to think of the emotional support provided by doulas as a way to avoid a mood disorder such as postpartum depression, instead of getting clinical help with this type of problem. I want women to know that it is not a sign of failure to ask for additional resources and support in your community. Even if a mother (or father) is not having a diagnosable mood disorder, the first few weeks and months after having a baby are never what one expects and the changes demanded by becoming a parent are a great opportunity to turn any difficulties into personal growth.

Margaret Bergmann-Ness lives and practices in Seattle, WA.

Part 2
After Baby's Arrival

Chapter 3:
Welcome, Baby!

Ch. 3

Strolling through the baby section of the card store tends to give one the impression that the early days at home with a baby involve small feet, cuddles, and ducks. To be sure, they do (maybe minus the ducks), but there is a sort of disconnect between the merry cards you receive in the mail and the scene potentially playing out in your home. Somewhere between the precious moments spent gazing at tiny toes and plain old exhaustion is your new reality.

We all have ideas about what we'll feel like as we take up life with our new baby. Maybe you have vague, dreamy images of snuggling your newborn in the early morning hours: you are an optimist and enjoy greeting cards. Maybe you have darker visions of pacing a cold kitchen floor and watching the clock hands inch along: you will be pleasantly surprised. Moms agree that the time immediately following birth involves great adjustment and it is almost never what we expect it to be.

How can we prepare for something that will inevitably be other than what we envisioned? Margaret Bergmann-Ness says that getting ready for the transition into parenthood is paradoxical. She likens a mom trying to emotionally prepare for the postpartum weeks to a fetus preparing to be a newborn; it is impossible to know what awaits you on the other side of this passage.

For those of us who like to anticipate events and plan ahead, all hope is not lost. The pages that follow do not reveal well-kept secrets, but offer some information that may help you reflect on this special and very unusual time in your life. Bottom line: there is a big learning curve for this job. If you view it as a learning process and know that eventually you will feel more like an expert than a novice, it's less daunting. You're in the weeds for a little while but you'll soon be confident about your parenting and well-rested once again. Congratulations! You're a parent!

Tip:

Find a comfortable spot and set up a feeding area where you have some basic supplies nearby: a cordless phone, a snack, something to read, and tons of water, especially if you're breast-feeding. Newborns often drift off to sleep while eating and you could find yourself in one place for a while with a precious bundle in your arms.

Ch. 3

Feed me!

Right after you and your baby are introduced for the first time, he is going to skip the small talk and want only one thing: to eat. Babies only do a few things, but those activities reoccur at an almost mind-blowing rate. Eating and sleeping are at the top of the list; diaper changes are merely a byproduct of all the nourishment. Many moms choose to breast-feed their babies and most hospitals encourage and facilitate this. Whether you are breast-feeding or bottle-feeding, this will be your first learning experience with your baby; and remember, it's going to be as big a learning curve for him as for you.

One common misconception about breast-feeding is that since the body naturally produces milk and mothers have fed infants this way since time immemorial, somehow all we mothers have an innate ability to perform the task. That may be technically true if we were put to some kind of survival test, but the reality is that most moms find breast-feeding very challenging in the first few weeks. You may hear people talk about getting breast-feeding "established." It takes time to get up and running and it requires patience, perseverance through some initial discomfort (sore nipples!), and a willingness to be flexible.

For breast-feeding to get off to a great start and succeed, support is your best bet. This means that either in the hospital or at home (or both), you need a person nearby who can answer questions, get up close and personal to help with things like latch and positioning, and mostly reassure you that the baby is behaving normally and doing what she should be doing. Where breast-feeding is concerned, you cannot ask enough questions. Most hospitals have lactation consultants on staff, and you may find that your pediatrician's office has resources to help you at home, such as a referral for a visiting a nurse. Postpartum doulas are also available for breast-feeding support (see chapter X). Many new moms are most comfortable getting help from a relative or friend who has breast-fed.

Breast-feeding is a little harder to get comfortable with than bottle-feeding for reasons that go beyond the physical. Even if you have your favorite position down and your baby is filling diapers like a champ, you may find that it bothers you not to know how much milk she's really getting. Bottles are filled with liquid (expressed breast milk or formula) that can be measured in ounces; moms are very reassured when they see the bottle go from full to empty at the end of a feeding. Breast-feeding leaves a lot more to the imagination. The best reassurance that your baby is getting enough milk is to have her weighed. You can buy a scale that measures to the ounce if you're really driving yourself nuts or you can wait until your two-week appointment with your doctor. However you decide to manage it, know that every breast-feeding mom has the same ques-

For breast-feeding to get off to a great start and succeed, support is your best bet. Most hospitals have lactation consultants on staff, and many pediatrician's offices have resources to help you at home, such as a referral for a visiting a nurse.

Ch. 3

tion: is my baby getting enough milk? This way of feeding a baby can be incredibly rewarding and has a long list of health benefits, but it initially requires a leap of faith.

It is often helpful to track feeding times, duration (if you're breast-feeding), or amount (if you're bottle-feeding). Tracking this information helps you determine an emerging feeding schedule, and this type of record will be important if you need to seek assistance from a lactation consultant or your doctor. How much record-keeping you do regarding eating and diapers is up to you, but the feeding/diaper logs at the end of this chapter will get you through about a week. You may want to reproduce the pages or adapt the log to suit your needs if you want to continue with a system like this. The first two or three days are very atypical for a baby (they usually sleep a ton) and not an optimal time to try to observe patterns, so I would suggest beginning to use the logs once you get home and are getting "established."

At some point, many moms transition from exclusive breast-feeding to a middle ground, using breast pumps to express and store milk for use when they are not available. This combination feeding method offers the health benefits of breast milk with the flexibility for others to feed your baby. Returning to work is one reason moms pump and store milk. Others want a reserve on hand (breast milk freezes well and can be stored for up to three months) in case they want to catch a movie or run errands for a few hours without their baby. Many moms find that breast-feeding is more successful overall for them when they have some freedom and flexibility. Others prefer not to pump and to be on hand when baby needs to eat.

While pumping is quite effortless for some, it can be frustrating or dissatisfying for others. If you want to give this a try, you might consider renting a pump for a week or two before you commit to buying one. Most hospitals rent pumps by the week or month. You do not need to have this figured out before you have your baby or in the first week! There is plenty of time to work on feeding alternatives—you don't need a master plan right away. It is enough to think through how you would ideally like to feed your baby when the big day arrives.

Singing the Baby Blues

I recall being awake in my hospital bed early in the morning, my day-old daughter dozing on my chest. I watched the sun rise and thought about her arrival. I felt at that moment pure, essential joy unfettered by any other emotion. The wave of feeling was almost too much to bear. That moment passed into another and I soon found myself at home, beginning a life with this new baby. To my surprise, I cried each evening for no particular reason between 5:00 and 7:00 P.M. (she cried for no apparent reason between 9:00 and11:00 P.M. and fortunately, our mood swings did not coincide). These melancholy moments were an emotional mystery; torrents of tears tied to no clear cause, right on schedule. I had a classic case of the baby blues but I didn't know why.

Pregnancy prepares you for what unusually high hormone levels can do—estrogen levels during pregnancy are about a thousand times higher than when you are not pregnant—and we're no stranger to mood swings by the time we give birth. But the first two or three weeks after having a baby is a hormonal roller coaster unlike any

There is a lot going on in the first month postpartum, a lot to process and learn. Hormonal changes are a major reason moms experience the blues, so If you are feeling a bit topsy-turvy, don't overlook hormones as a culprit.

other. The changeability some of us experience is the result of a precipitous fall in levels of estrogen and progesterone. Logic would dictate that if your hormones can make it possible for a human being to grow in your body and then get born, those hormones have to go somewhere and do something once that baby has departed. It's odd that nobody really seems to mention it much during pregnancy but, after all, there is so much else to talk about then.

It's not really such a scary thing if you just think of it as your body decompressing after a marathon experience. Some relaxed, happy

. . . .

The postpartum period is often called the fourth trimester for good reason: you are letting go of pregnancy and your birth experience and moving into motherhood gradually. At the same time, your baby is experiencing her own "fourth trimester" adjusting to life outside the comforts of the womb.

. . . .

moments, some tears, nothing terribly extreme. But many new moms feel alarmed by the ups and downs, the tears, or whatever form the decompression takes. Some moms feel it's wrong to be weepy or short-fused when such a joyous event has taken place and they feel a sense of guilt for any emotion that isn't 100 percent positive. Although the birth of a child is a celebratory time, it is also complicated and there are real causes for feeling "blue." Here's the good news: mood swings, by definition, have an upside and the

highs can be out of the stratosphere, the stuff that dreams are made of.

In *The Post-Pregnancy Handbook*, Sylvia Brown reports that 70 to 80 percent of new moms experience a harmless form of depression between the third and eleventh day after giving birth. Not to be confused with postpartum depression, the blues last about two weeks. Brown says that for many moms who give birth in a hospital, the tears often start flowing the day you return home. This is because you are now in a private environment where you can relax and be yourself and also because you have just left the support system of a hospital where you could summon an expert with the push of a button. When returning home, many moms get overwhelmed and experience a "first day of the rest of my life" feeling.

There is a lot going on in the first month postpartum, a lot to process and learn. Of course, as I already mentioned, hormonal changes are a major reason moms experience the blues. If you feel a bit topsy-turvy,

Ch. 3

don't overlook hormones as a culprit.

Other reasons new moms get blue are feelings of uncertainty or a lack of self-confidence. This may mean that you think your visiting mother or mother-in-law diapers better than you do and that you are therefore lesser in some way. It may mean that you

....

The bonding that takes place between a baby and mother is not always instantaneous. Don't worry if maternal instincts don't spring from every pore the moment your baby is in your arms. One devoted mom of three said of connecting with her firstborn, "I felt like I was babysitting for the first month". If you don't feel an instant bond, it will come in time as you continue to care for and get to know your baby.

....

even have some regrets, that you wonder at times what you've gotten yourself into. If you are feeling uncertain about either your abilities as a parent or your decision to become one, you are not alone. And you will gain confidence as the days pass. Soon you will be the resident expert. Some moms also experience anxiety about the baby's fragility or vulnerability. This comes up a lot when it is time to bathe your baby. It's normal to have a fear of dropping your baby or bathing her incorrectly. It's a scary proposition to have such a tiny person in your arms and to make her all wet and slippery! This too takes practice and confidence builds. Be patient with yourself; no expert was ever created overnight.

Another possible cause of the blues stems from the event that just took place: you have given birth. Many moms do not have the birth experience they envisioned and it takes some time to reflect on your baby's birth and work through it. Although

Ch. 3

Brown points out that baby blues affect moms regardless of what their childbirth experience has been, we must acknowledge that especially if your birth experience was not what you envisioned, you may need some time to talk about what you expected and how the experience surprised you in some way. And although everyone says "all I want is a healthy baby" and it is, of course, the truth, it doesn't mean you will be able to gloss over any disappointments that giving birth brought for you. It is perfectly acceptable to feel disappointed for a little while if you labored for twenty-six hours and ended up with an emergency C-Section. And it's perfectly acceptable to feel blue if you were in labor for 3 hours and had the birth of your dreams. The point is, this is not a time to feel guilty about the feelings you have or believe that your emotions are inappropriate or somehow out of place. Have them. Talk about them. And remember that this is a stage—a fourth trimester of sorts—and you will not feel this way for long.

The baby blues is not an illness and can be alleviated with rest and support from loved ones, whereas postpartum depression requires treatment. If you believe you may have postpartum depression, seek the advice of your doctor or midwife.

When the Blues Do Not Blow Over

How do you know if you have a mild—and common—case of the baby blues or a more serious condition known as postpartum depression? About one in ten women experience a depression that begins sometime during the first year after birth and requires treatment. Treatment for postpartum depression can include therapy, medication, or alternative remedies. Postpartum depression is an illness and will not simply go

Some common symptoms of the baby blues and postpartum depression

Baby Blues	Postpartum Depression
Feeling exhausted, overwhelmed Fitful sleep and unusual sleep patterns	Tired all the time, lethargic, sleep brings no relief Sleeping during the day, insomnia at night
Frequent changes in mood	Fits of anger and irritability
Frustration, irritability, anxiety	Anxiety attacks
Difficulty concentrating	Great difficulty concentrating: forget even very important things
Feeling of slow bonding with new baby	Feeling numb toward baby, distant from partner
Concern about competence to care for baby	Feeling cut off from the world Lack of self-esteem, feeling unwanted
Heightened sensitivity to advice/criticism	Feeling paralyzed, overwhelmed
Tears for seemingly minor reasons	Persistent sadness
	Frightening recurring thoughts including feelings of a desire to harm yourself or your baby Lack of appetite

Ch. 3

away as time passes. If you have this condition, you will need to ask for help.

Since symptoms of postpartum depression are often more severe manifestations of baby blues complaints, it's easy to wonder about this distinction. The clearest differentiation I have found is made by Tracy Hogg in *Secrets of the Baby Whisperer*. She characterizes the

Ch. 3

baby blues as a time of powerful mood swings. As long as there are in fact swings, meaning that you have your joy and tenderness toward your baby mixed with tears and irritability, then you have a textbook case of the blues. It's when a persistent sadness lingers or you fail to periodically swing back up that you have cause for concern. Hogg suggests keeping a journal to monitor your mood swings. You can use some of the blank pages at the back of this book to note moods and changes in how you feel.

It is very likely that as you get more rest and physically recover from giving birth, you'll feel more like yourself and any doubts about whether you have postpartum depression will vanish. If you continue to have doubts about your mental (or physical) well-being, there is no harm in consulting your obstetrician, midwife, therapist or other health practitioner. Giving birth takes a toll on body and mind and you should seek the level of support you need.

Resources

Baby Care:

Books:

• *The Baby Book: Everything You Need to Know About Your Baby from Birth to Age Two* by Dr. William Sears.

• *Your Baby and Child: From Birth to Age Five* by Penelope Leach

• *The Girlfriend's Guide to Surviving the First Year of Motherhood* by Vicki Iovine

• *The Secrets of the Baby Whisperer: How to Calm, Connect and Communicate with Your Baby* by Tracy Hogg

• *The Happiest Baby on the Block* by Dr. Harvey Karp

• *Touchpoints: Your Child's Emotional and Behavioral Development: Birth-Age 3* by T. Berry Brazelton

• *What to Expect the First Year* by Heidi Murkoff et. al.

Online:

• **National Dissemination Center for Children with Disabilities:** www.nichcy.org

• For links and resources when expecting multiples: www.twinslist.org

• **Baby Center:** www.babycenter.com

• **Zero to Three:** www.zerotothree.org

Breast-feeding

Books:

• *The Breast-feeding Book: Everything You Need to Know About Nursing Your Child from Birth Through Weaning,* by Martha Sears, RN and Dr. William Sears.

• *Mothering Multiples: Breast-feeding & Caring for Twins or More,* by Karen Kerkhoff Gromada, La Leche League International, 1999

• *The Nursing Mother's Companion,* by Kathleen Huggins, Harvard Common Press, 1999. This book has a very helpful section on selecting a breast pump.

• *Nursing Mother, Working Mother: The Essential Guide for Breast-feeding and Staying Close to Your Baby After You Return to Work* by Gale Pryor, Harvard Common Press 1997

• *The Womanly Art of Breast-feeding,* La Leche League International

• *The Ultimate Breast-feeding Book of Answers: The Most Comprehensive Problem-Solution Guide to Breast-feeding from the Foremost Expert in North America,* by Jack Newman MD, Teresa Pitman

Online:

• La Leche League
www.lalecheleague.org

• Medela, Inc. (Pumps)
www.medela.com

Baby Blues, Postpartum Concerns and Depression

Print:

• *Conquering Postpartum Depression: A Proven Plan for Recovery,* Ronald Rosenberg, M.D.

• *The New Mother's Body Book* by Jacqueline Shannon

• *The Post-Pregnancy Handbook* by Sylvia Brown and Mary Dowd Struck

• *This Isn't What I Expected: Overcoming Postpartum Depression,* by Karen R. Kleiman and Valerie Raskin

Online:

• Depression After Delivery (DAD)
www.depressionafterdelivery.com
800-944-4773 (4PPD)

• Postpartum Assistance for Mothers (PAM)
510-727-4610

Ch. 3

Tips on using the feeding and diapering log

- If you use one sheet for more than one 24-hour cycle, you can use a symbol such as # in the date column to indicate a new day.
- If you are record-keeping for more than one baby, use alternating sheets and label each sheet with the baby's name.

- Consider using the notes column to record information such as a baby's weight or something else you may need to keep track of.
- This sheet was designed to be concise: in no way do diaper changes need to coincide with feedings. When using the diaper portion of the chart, come up with a system that works for you, such as creating another date/time column on the far right side of the page.

Ch. 3

Tips on using the food intake log

Breast milk When very young infants are cranky and cannot be comforted, breast-feeding moms often begin to suspect that a food they are eating may be the culprit. For some babies dairy is an irritant and for others it can be something very specific like chocolate. You can use this space to try to observe a connection between a particular food and your baby's discomfort. Make as complete a list of foods consumed as you can in any given day. You may want to make additional logs of your own if this becomes a long process or just use this page to make a few notes.

Formula Babies drinking formula occasionally have an allergic reaction as well. There are an array of formulas on the market, including non-dairy options. If you suspect that your baby may be having a reaction to his formula, you can make observations by using just the date and notes columns.

Feeding and Diapering Log

Date	Time	Started on		Duration		Ounces	Diaper contents	Notes
		Breast-feeding				**Bottle-feeding**	**Diaper Record**	
		Started on		Duration		Ounces	Diaper contents	Notes
	AM/PM	Left	Right	Left	Right			
	AM/PM	Left	Right	Left	Right			
	AM/PM	Left	Right	Left	Right			
	AM/PM	Left	Right	Left	Right			
	AM/PM	Left	Right	Left	Right			
	AM/PM	Left	Right	Left	Right			
	AM/PM	Left	Right	Left	Right			
	AM/PM	Left	Right	Left	Right			
	AM/PM	Left	Right	Left	Right			
	AM/PM	Left	Right	Left	Right			
	AM/PM	Left	Right	Left	Right			
	AM/PM	Left	Right	Left	Right			

Ch. 3

Observations and Questions: _____

_____

_____

Feeding and Diapering Log

Date	Time	Breast-feeding Started on	Breast-feeding Duration	Bottle-feeding Ounces	Diaper Record Diaper contents	Notes
	AM/PM	Left Right	Left Right			
	AM/PM	Left Right	Left Right			
	AM/PM	Left Right	Left Right			
	AM/PM	Left Right	Left Right			
	AM/PM	Left Right	Left Right			
	AM/PM	Left Right	Left Right			
	AM/PM	Left Right	Left Right			
	AM/PM	Left Right	Left Right			
	AM/PM	Left Right	Left Right			
	AM/PM	Left Right	Left Right			
	AM/PM	Left Right	Left Right			
	AM/PM	Left Right	Left Right			

Observations and Questions: _____

_____

_____

Ch. 3

Feeding and Diapering Log

| Date | Time | Breast-feeding | | Bottle-feeding | Diaper Record | |
		Started on	Duration	Ounces	Diaper contents	Notes
	AM/PM	Left Right	Left Right			
	AM/PM	Left Right	Left Right			
	AM/PM	Left Right	Left Right			
	AM/PM	Left Right	Left Right			
	AM/PM	Left Right	Left Right			
	AM/PM	Left Right	Left Right			
	AM/PM	Left Right	Left Right			
	AM/PM	Left Right	Left Right			
	AM/PM	Left Right	Left Right			
	AM/PM	Left Right	Left Right			
	AM/PM	Left Right	Left Right			
	AM/PM	Left Right	Left Right			

Ch. 3

Observations and Questions: _____

_____

_____

Food Intake Sheet

Date	Foods consumed	Notes
	Breakfast: Lunch: Dinner: Snacks:	
	Breakfast: Lunch: Dinner: Snacks:	
	Breakfast: Lunch: Dinner: Snacks:	
	Breakfast: Lunch: Dinner: Snacks:	
	Breakfast: Lunch: Dinner: Snacks:	

Find this worksheet online at www.babyfilebook.com

Ch. 3

Date	Foods consumed	Notes
	Breakfast: Lunch: Dinner: Snacks:	
	Breakfast: Lunch: Dinner: Snacks:	
	Breakfast: Lunch: Dinner: Snacks:	
	Breakfast: Lunch: Dinner: Snacks:	
	Breakfast: Lunch: Dinner: Snacks:	

Ch
3

Ask an Expert

Maria Burtis is the mother of Eloise, 4, and Theo, 2. In our talk she shares some recollections about motherhood and offers some tips for new parents.

Q **So, the question on every woman's mind is: What do you wish someone had told you about new motherhood before the baby was born?**

A *Well, I remember when I was pregnant I thought I knew exactly what I would want in the first weeks after giving birth. I thought Andy [Maria's husband] and I would want a lot of privacy. I didn't want to book up our calendar with visitors and didn't like the idea of having a house full of people.*

When Eloise was born and I was at home with her, what I actually wanted was constant companionship. I wanted someone to sit on the couch with me for hours. I needed a certain kind of support that only came from someone being around. So my first advice is to be as flexible as you can—that's hard when people have to buy plane tickets but play it by ear because you may not actually want what you think you wanted and that's okay.

Q **Can you give me two or three more?**

A *Another thing I recall feeling is that nursing was not as easy and natural as I expected. Nursing can be tough and I assumed it would be easy. I never even thought about it beforehand. I wished I had had some information about what to do to feed a hungry baby if your milk comes in late or if you are engorged. I ended up sitting in my foyer with my neighbor while she helped me use a breast pump to relieve the engorged situation. I didn't have formula in the house, but I wouldn't even have known how much to feed a newborn.*

Also, in the hospital we got massively conflicting advice on things like swaddling, using a pacifier, and co-sleeping. Andy had a great suggestion. He said we needed to "listen for the gold" and tune out everything else. One nurse would tell us one thing and the next had a different point of view. We just tried to keep listening for what felt right for us.

What was the happiest moment you experienced early on?

I think it would have been on the second day in the hospital and having her sleep on me—I had my legs bent so she could sleep on me and I was just staring at her and it was the first time I got to really look at her. I looked at her little fingers and she was so peaceful and quiet. She was wearing her little cap and all wrapped up in a blanket.

For Andy the greatest moment was when he was up late at night with her and it was dark. She had her eyes wide open and she was reaching out for his face.

What were your initial feelings about your baby?

I was terrified that the baby would stop breathing. I used to go into her room all the time to check on her.

I still do!

And I'm a responsible person, someone who's always on the hook. But when she was born I felt really on the hook and that I couldn't quit ever and the incredible responsibility the relationship brought. The rewards were also huge right away. The connectedness—and I contemplated the awesome nature of the relationship.

There was one night during our first week home when I was sitting at the table and Andy's whole family was there too. Eloise was sleeping right near the table and I couldn't focus on anyone at the table because I had to keep looking at her. Every two seconds I had to look at her. And when I looked away from her I felt so relieved—that's terrible to say but I did. Then I would look back again.

Ch.
3

Did you feel how you expected to feel after giving birth?

I don't know what I expected but I feel like I knew about some of the physical stuff like bleeding for a while, not wanting to have sex for a while, but I didn't know about nightsweats and I didn't know about the crying. Now I know it all happens for a reason and that your hormones are rebalancing. At the time I was so surprised how teary I was and how much crying I did. I knew I wasn't depressed but there was so much strong feeling. And I felt so much shame about being sad! It didn't occur to me until much later that exhaustion can lead to tears, too.

When did you start thinking of yourself as a mother?

I don't know—not while I was pregnant. It came on gradually, it was a becoming process. Now I feel like a mother but I can't pinpoint the time.

I feel the same way. I feel so totally in the role now but I'm not sure when or how that happened.

In what ways did you feel sure of yourself as a mother?

That I wouldn't be afraid forever and that I wouldn't be a mother who was overly anxious or worried. I knew then that on some level I knew what was best for her. I became more open to inviting people in and listening to their advice because I knew I was doing a good job.

What does it feel like to be really sleep deprived?

Like finals week except that there's no pint of Ben and Jerry's at the end! There's no endpoint in sight. It's not one all-nighter or even like if in college you did something really crazy and pulled two all-nighters. Everyone reacts differently to it and I thought that everything seemed so hard. Walking to the kitchen to make a sandwich was hard. I was living in disorder and I so badly wanted to clean it all up but the mess was pretty insurmountable, or it felt that way. Some people get angry, some cry a lot. I just felt really spacey all the time and don't have a clear, sharp memory of that time.

How do you relax as a new mom?

Baths are great. You can go on an auditory vacation from the baby when you run the water because you can't hear any noises. Even if Andy and the baby were in the next room I couldn't hear them in the tub. There's something about a bath—the rhythm of the water. Plus if you have a vaginal delivery you sometimes take sitz baths to heal and it feels great to fill a whole bath and soak.

Another thing is to have someone else take the baby for a walk so you can be in your own space and have no demands on you. You can read or whatever you want with no baby around.

Is there anything you want to add?

Yes. Don't try to figure out sleep stuff in the middle of the night! If you have a plan, stick to your plan at 3:00 A.M. and talk to your partner the next day. Make your goals—if you have goals—in the daylight hours and they can be revised after a rough night but don't try to make changes in the middle of it all or question things in the night.

And think long and hard about what you want long-term. Begin as you mean to carry on.

But a lot of people say that habits aren't really formed until much later.

That's true but you have to keep the big picture in mind. Realize that if you have a goal, it's not achievable in a day or a week, but ask yourself if you're using a pacifier, do you want to be using one at five months? At eight months? At a year? And if you keep the grander goals in mind then you can make it all happen bit by bit.

Chapter 4:
Sleep

Once you've settled in at home with your baby, your thoughts may rapidly turn to sleep—yours and your baby's. Newborn babies sleep between16 and 20 hours a day. If the wee ones opted for 20 consecutive hours, the weeks following a baby's arrival would be a time of rest and relaxation. But alas, as we know, they tend to slumber sporadically, wake at unpredictable intervals, and even appear nocturnal at times. It's a good thing they are so darn cute.

The good news is, this is a relatively short-lived phase. Every baby has his or her own patterns and parents have very different expectations about how sleep should be achieved. Generally though, sleep as a topic takes center stage for every family in the first few months. Then, slowly but surely, the focus changes to other areas of development. Take comfort in the fact that parents of older babies are usually chatting about things other than how much sleep they got the night before. It's on to solids, childproofing, and potty seats. You too will breathe a sigh of relief some fine day and eventually have to search your memory to recall the unique torment of being awakened every few hours.

This chapter will help you navigate the vast array of sleep resources awaiting you at the bookstore or library. When you reach the parenting section, you will find hundreds of books from floor to ceiling, and somewhere in the stacks may be your key to elusive slumber. Take comfort in this too. If there are more books on sleep than you could peruse in a lifetime, a few others must be up at night as well—and never has misery loved company as much as a group of sleep-deprived parents. You can use this cheat sheet on popular sleep approaches to narrow your search and have some authors and titles in mind for your pilgrimage.

Ch.
4

The Sleep Debate

Sleep is one of the most hotly debated areas of parenting. As you grow into your parenting role, you'll find it is almost impossible not to form a strong opinion about sleep. Sleep experts agree that sleep is essential for babies to grow and develop and most would say that, due to biological factors, it takes a minimum of six weeks for sleep patterns to begin to get organized. Many experts who offer sleep training techniques suggest beginning at about four months due to the fact that babies do not have the memory or the organization to benefit from sleep training prior to that point. And that's about where the agreement ends.

The crux of the sleep issue is the question of assisted sleep versus unassisted sleep, how to achieve it, and at what age. Put another way, how do you plan to help

....

Be careful about assuming that your baby is a "bad sleeper" and needs less sleep than other babies. Dr. Richard Ferber cautions that although babies have different sleep needs, if you make this kind of assumption early on, you may influence behavior and miss opportunities to help your child develop good sleep habits. Hold off on any judgment and keep trying to help your baby get as much sleep as possible.

....

your baby fall asleep and how early do you want her to learn to fall asleep on her own? Babies must not only learn to put themselves to sleep initially, but help themselves return to sleep if they awaken during the night. Learning to return to sleep without any assistance or intervention from you is the key to sleeping through the night.

Some parents believe in (or resort to) teaching their babies how to sleep independently by employing a sleep training method and others are content to forgo any particular method and wait for a child to develop this ability on his own. The plan you start out with may or may not lead to the desired result. It's also likely that what fits at two months may not fit at seven months. Helping a baby learn to sleep is a dynamic process and it's important to be flexible and try new approaches as needed.

Sleep approaches fall into two main camps: parent-directed and attachment parenting. Then there is the middle ground, of course, which is where many of us are likely

These approaches sound straight-forward when you don't have an actual baby to consider—that is, when they're theoretical. I thought I was clear on where I stood before my daughter was born. I had to reevaluate. Then my son was born and I had to reevaluate again. It just wasn't as simple as saying "this is what I believe" and watching my kids fall in line. My core beliefs never changed, but the way I have approached helping two babies learn to sleep has been very different and I've had to be more flexible than I imagined.

part of it, not the other way around. In short, parents are at the helm and decide when a baby eats and sleeps. Attachment parenting allows a child's rhythms and expression of needs to primarily dictate when events like eating and sleeping take place.

Parent-directed approaches, which often include some crying it out, advocate unassisted sleep as early as possible. Proponents argue that learning to fall asleep independently fosters self-confidence. While it may be difficult to listen to your child crying, ultimately you are helping your child; teaching your child to achieve independent sleep is part of your care for her, just like feeding and bathing.

The attachment parenting approach to sleep, which is almost synonymous with the name Dr. William Sears, argues that a crying infant is expressing a need and the need must be met to ensure trust develops between parent and child. Trust ultimately fosters self-esteem. In response to what Dr. Sears calls "restrained response" parenting,

Ch. 4

to end up. These philosophies extend far beyond sleep; they impact all areas of child-rearing. Parent-directed approaches believe that a baby joins a household and becomes

he writes, "Independence is not, in itself, one of our most important parenting goals. It is not the parents' responsibility to make a child independent but rather to create a secure environment and a feeling of right-ness which allows a child's independence to develop naturally."

Let's tell it like it is: the sleep debate is values-laden and you will have to figure out what is best for your baby and your family.

What are your expectations about your baby's sleep? Where should a baby sleep? In a crib in her own room, in a bassinet in your room, in your bed? And ask yourself how you feel about crying. Is a crying infant expressing a need that should be met right away or is it okay to let a baby cry some-times? What circumstances, such as returning to work, may influence the sleep approaches you try?

What the Experts are Saying
(This list is not comprehensive)

Parent-directed	Middle Ground	Attachment Parenting
• Ezzo, *On Becoming Baby Wise* • Ferber, *Solve your Child's Sleep Problems* • Mindell, *Sleeping Through the Night* • Weissbluth, *Healthy Sleep Habits, Happy Child* • Wilkoff, *Is My Child Overtired?: The Sleep Solution for Raising Happier, Healthier Children*	• Brazelton, *Sleep: The Brazelton Way* • Cuthbertson/Schevill, *Helping Your Child Sleep Through the Night* • Hogg, *The Secrets of the Baby Whisperer* • Karp, *The Happiest Baby on the Block* • Leach, *Your Baby and Child*	• Gordon/Goodavage, *Good Nights: The Happy Parents' Guide to the Family Bed (and a Peaceful Night's Sleep)* • Pantley, *The No-Cry Sleep Solution: Gentle Ways to Help Your Baby Sleep Through the Night* • Sears, *Nighttime Parenting*

Ch. 4

Parent-Directed Approaches

Dr. Richard Ferber:
Solve your Child's Sleep Problems

The approach:

For several decades, Dr. Ferber's approach has been synonymous with letting babies "cry it out." "Ferberizing," as the sleep training technique is often called, is based on the premise that children need to learn to fall asleep on their own without their parents in the room. While crying it out is an oversimplification of his method, his plan includes some tears for sure. The crying is the result of timed waiting intervals which are the centerpiece of the technique. When you begin the training you let your baby cry for five minutes and then return to his room to reassure with your voice. Then you exit again and wait ten minutes this time. Intervals get increasingly longer until the baby falls asleep. The next night you begin with a ten minute interval and work up from there. This method is used at nap time and bedtime.

In the 2006 revision of his book, *Solve Your Child's Sleep Problems*, Dr. Ferber has modified his approach and softened his perspective a bit: he now advocates a variety of techniques for helping babies fall asleep. In an effort to clarify his theory, he acknowledges that there is no magic solution for getting a child to sleep and that different problems call for different solutions.

Age when independent sleep can be achieved:

All babies 4 to 6 months of age can learn to sleep well and on their own. Prior to 4–6 months of age, any sleep ritual that works is fine, such as rocking or using a pacifier to help a baby fall asleep.

Practical guide or general philosophy?

Dr. Ferber's book is a practical sleep training guide, reassuring parents that no matter how frustrated they may be, there is a way to identify a sleep problem and then solve it in clear, easy steps. His concrete advice speaks to many a tired parent's desire for a series of practical steps to change their baby's sleep behavior. In other words, he offers what can potentially be a quick fix to an overwhelming issue.

Dr. Marc Weissbluth:
Healthy Sleep Habits, Happy Child

Ch. 4

The approach:

Dr. Weissbluth views healthy sleep habits and good rest as the key to happy, calm, alert children. According to Weissbluth, the goal for parents is to do things that respect your child's need to sleep and not do things that interfere with the natural sleep process. He suggests that we parents need to do a good job of protecting our children's need to sleep.

One of Weissbluth's mantras is that "sleep begets sleep." It is much harder to soothe and calm an overtired baby than a well-rested baby.

Dr. Weissbluth states that "Making children cry is not the way to help them learn to sleep." Some crying may be a by-product of his sleep training technique, but the focus of the technique is on timing, motionless sleep, and consistency in soothing/sleeping style (on the part of the parents). Motionless sleep simply means that stationary sleep is more restful than sleep in a swing or car, etc. Consistency in soothing style suggests that parents should choose a style of putting a baby down to sleep and stick with it to help the baby learn how it's done.

Although Dr. Weissbluth's sleep training technique does not rely on crying it out as a method, you will find some tough love in the approach. For example, if you are trying to wean your baby off a night feed at five or six months of age, he advises against going to a crying baby in the middle of the night. There are no timed waiting intervals, no voice to reassure, as in Dr. Ferber's approach.

Age when independent sleep can be achieved:

Although Dr. Weissbluth says that learning to fall asleep is something that happens naturally, healthy sleep habits do not develop naturally and this is what parents must teach their babies. After several weeks of age, parents can shape natural sleep rhythms into good sleep habits. By 3 to 4 months of age, babies should be falling asleep on their own and have some self-soothing habits to put themselves back to sleep if they awaken at night.

Practical guide or general philosophy?

In *Healthy Sleep Habits, Happy Child,* Dr. Weissbluth offers parents guidelines for helping babies establish good sleep habits. You will not find a step-by-step plan but Weissbluth makes his rationale and goal quite clear. You might have to be a little creative figuring out how to get there.

Ch. 4

The Middle-Ground

Practitioners whose approaches fall into the middle-ground believe that babies need to learn to sleep on their own and that independent sleep should be achieved as soon as possible for the benefit of the entire family. However, this group will not recommend achieving the goal at any cost: letting a baby cry it out is not a strategy or by-product of these approaches.

Tracy Hogg:
The Secrets of the Baby Whisperer

The approach:

Hogg's book presents her complete baby-care regimen, EASY., which covers all aspects of life with a newborn, including sleep. With the acronym E = Eating, A = Activity, S = Sleep, and Y = Your time, EASY is based on the premise that babies' behavior offers cues to their needs. By following your baby's cues, it is possible to create a schedule that has benefits for both baby and parents. Babies will be well-rested and well-fed, parents will actually have some time to themselves. EASY is a middle-ground between a rigid schedule and on-demand feeding.

In Hogg's approach, which she calls "sensible sleep," a parent must learn to recognize the signs of sleepiness and act accordingly. The crux of the approach is timing. Hogg describes three stages as a baby passes into sleep: the "window," the "zone," and "letting go." During what she calls the "window," for example, a baby exhibits "sleepytime signs" such as turning her face away from objects and people. Hogg takes readers step by step through her approach and leaves no doubt about how to learn cues and implement "sensible sleep."

Age when independent sleep can be achieved:

Hogg suggests working toward independent sleep from day one. In her words, "Begin as you mean to carry on." It is important to respect your baby and learn about his cues, all the while creating a framework in which parents can exist happily and babies sleep well on their own.

> Hogg helps moms to break the cycle of eating and falling asleep by separating feeding from sleep. This is the key to being able to take a shower, do a load of laundry and have something to eat.

Practical guide or general philosophy?

Parents often wish aloud for operating instructions. Well, Hogg's book is the closest I've found. You will find a clear philosophy laid out, one that respects the rights of parents to maintain their own lives, and a tender perspective on the little ones who join our lives. Along with an explanation of this philosophy, there is abundant and detailed advice that takes you from your arrival at home to a time when babies and parents alike sleep through the night.

Dr. Harvey Karp:
The Happiest Baby on the Block

The approach:

Dr. Karp's book, *The Happiest Baby on the Block*, does not focus solely on sleep, but rather on how to calm crying babies and in so doing, help them sleep better and longer. The cornerstone of his approach is the five S's: swaddling, side/stomach position (in your arms, not in a crib), shushing, swinging and sucking. Dr. Karp has found that these strategies, when used in combination, have an amazing calming effect on even the fussiest babies.

He devotes one chapter of his book to the "magical 6th 'S'," sleep. His approach toward sleep training is extremely gentle. He says "I encourage you to respond to your tiny baby's needs with promptness and love . . . The bottom line is that your job as a parent is to adapt to the needs of your newborn, not the other way around." He does, however, recognize that a schedule can be beneficial for both parents and infants and suggests ways to begin implementing a schedule if you are so inclined. He also describes in detail how to wean your baby off the five S's over time so that he develops the ability to fall asleep—and stay asleep—on his own.

Surprisingly, Dr. Karp's approach has something to offer both the parent who wants to create order in a chaotic time and parents who have no interest in schedules but have a keen interest in a tranquil infant. His approach is about calming: a code every parent wants to crack.

Age when independent sleep can be achieved:

This varies based on an infant's ability to mold to a schedule. Some infants do well when put on a schedule as early as one to two months and others do not. Dr. Karp explains that this has to do with an infant's ability to handle delayed gratification. Because Dr. Karp is also an advocate of co-sleeping if a family desires it, he doesn't offer an age at which a child should be sleeping on her own, unassisted.

Practical guide or general philosophy?

Dr. Karp's advice is extremely practical. In fact, his method is based on performing the five S's exactly right and in the right order. While having a manual to follow can be just the ticket if it's the middle of the night and your baby is inconsolable, your angst may increase if your baby continues crying and you feel you're "doing it wrong." What you gain in concrete advice in this resource has a downside: what to do if the miracle fix just doesn't work for you?

Attachment Parenting

Dr. William Sears: Nighttime Parenting

The approach:

The very name of Dr. Sears' book on sleep, *Nighttime Parenting*, speaks volumes about his approach: parents play an integral part in helping a baby fall asleep. Because

Sears is also an advocate of co-sleeping, or sharing a family bed, it follows that parents would already be present to help infants return to sleep.

Sears' approach to helping an infant sleep relies on parental assistance, which includes nursing, swaddling, rocking, rhythmic patting, womb sounds/white noise, and many other ideas outlined in his books.

Dr. Sears views attachment parenting as a way of following intuition and natural responses. A baby's cries are designed to activate a mother's response. And an infant's cries are more than just a trigger to a maternal response: crying is a baby's language, however basic. This is the baby's communication network and a baby cries because he is communicating a need. The early weeks with an infant are about establishing a parent-baby communication network.

Sears firmly denounces the cry-it-out technique, saying that this behaviorist approach is trying to extinguish a habit (night waking), but in actuality, night waking is not a habit but a need. He is unequivocal: crying it out is detrimental for the entire family, especially for a mother and baby.

Age when independent sleep can be achieved:

This varies based on an individual child and unassisted sleep is not a goal in and of itself.

Practical guide or general philosophy?

Sears writes, "Difficult problems in child-rearing do not have easy answers." In his many books on baby care, you will not find step-by-step programs to get to a goal but a philosophy for parenting and suggestions on how to cope with various challenges that arise when caring for a baby.

 Elizabeth Pantley's *The No-Cry Sleep Solution* is a relative newcomer on the scene and has been welcomed by many a parent who is looking to avoid crying it out but also looking for some practical tips. Pantley's book is endorsed by Sears and really goes into

Ch. 4

amazing detail to walk parents through the steps of helping babies learn to sleep. Pantley includes plans for babies in cribs and co-sleeping babies. If it's a manual you're after, run, don't walk to your nearest bookstore and get yourself a copy.

Below are some tips on sleep gathered from collective mom wisdom and experience:

- **Sleep is challenging for every family with a new baby. You are not alone in your sleeplessness.**

- **Sleep when the baby sleeps. You've heard it a thousand times but it bears repeating. Your friends and family will happily wait for your return calls, e-mail and thank-you notes.**

- **Tag-team with your partner. Get some rest when you're off duty. Consider ear plugs so you can really tune out for an hour or two.**

- **You may not currently have a philosophy about sleep but you will develop one (consciously or not) as you go along. Your beliefs about sleep may go through several revisions before you hit upon the magic ritual that works for your baby. Be open to change and trying new things.**

- **Always trust your instincts and do what feels right for you and your baby.**

- **By week two or three you may be consumed with schemes to help your baby sleep longer and that is absolutely normal. But try not to develop these plans during the night. Regroup in the light of day.**

- **Keeping a sleep diary helps you recognize emerging patterns. You may want to make some notes about sleep patterns on page X or tailor it to better suit your purposes. It works best once sleep gets more organized: after 3 to 4 months.**

- **A well-rested baby is not the only concern here: make sleep and food your top two priorities. Staying hydrated is especially important if you're breast-feeding.**

**Ch.
4**

So venture forth and find yourself a few good sleep resources. Please remember that you don't have to decide on an approach immediately. Your baby is going to continue to grow and develop. Part of what we parents do is adapt to the ever-evolving needs of our babies and keep our minds open to new possibilities.

notes:_____

_____

_____

_____

_____

_____

_____

_____

_____

_____

Ch.
4

Why do babies wake up during the night?

In *Nighttime Parenting*, Dr. Sears offers some clues to nightime waking:

Physical Causes:

- Hungry
- Wet
- Too hot or too cold
- Teething
- Developmental milestones such as grabbing or rolling over (may wake the baby up as he practices in his sleep)

Environmental Causes:

- Room temperature too hot or cold (or marked temperature fluctuation) 70 degrees is preferable.
- Noise: during the first few months babies are easily aroused by light and touch.

Medical Causes:

- Stuffy nose
- Allergies
- Reflux (similar to heartburn in adults)

Sleep Diary

Many sleep experts suggest keeping a sleep diary. A sleep diary can make patterns evident that you may not be aware of. This type of log is ideally begun at about 3 to 4 months when a baby's daytime and nighttime sleep becomes more organized. It is most beneficial to keep a sleep diary for a minimum of one week and probably best to shoot for two. There are many advantages to tracking sleep habits:

1. Once you record sleep and observe a pattern, you can plan your day in such a way that you make napping possible at certain times of day, ensuring that your efforts to help your baby fall asleep coincide with your baby's natural inclination to sleep at particular intervals. A sleep diary will help ensure that you are working with your baby's biological sleep rhythm and not against it.

2. If you are struggling with some aspect of sleep, the diary is a handy record to bring along to your regular doctor visits. You may

Ch. 4

not remember the specifics when asked because you will have been up at night so much! Your doctor can look at your diary and help you fine-tune your baby's bedtime or discuss various sleep strategies and techniques.

3. If you track your baby's sleep and your three-month-old's total sleep in a 24-hour cycle is, say, 10 hours, you'll be able to compare this with the norm for his age, then perhaps set a goal to help him take more frequent naps. Your sleep log will allow you to record experiments, such as a nap at an earlier time or an extra nap, and then write down the results of that change.

Below is a sample sleep diary. The charts are blank so you can fine-tune the categories to best suit your needs. Use the blank pages at the back of the book if you need more space.

Sleep Diary	Sun	Mon	Tues	Wed	Thurs	Fri	Sat
Time of waking							
Time /duration of naps							
Total daytime sleep							
Time baby was put to bed							
Time baby fell asleep							
Time of night waking (s)							
Action taken during night wakings							
Total nighttime sleep							
Notes							

Sleep Diary	Sun	Mon	Tues	Wed	Thurs	Fri	Sat

Ch.
4

Sleep Diary	Sun	Mon	Tues	Wed	Thurs	Fri	Sat

Ch. 4

Sleep Diary	Sun	Mon	Tues	Wed	Thurs	Fri	Sat

Ch.
4

Ask an Expert

Dr. Will Wilkoff, pediatrician and sleep expert

Q **For new parents, what would you say is the most common misconception about sleep?**

A *Hmmm, that's a good question. One of them is that on the one hand they've heard how often babies get up at night and that they're going to have a rough time with sleep and on the other hand, parents often underestimate how much a baby should be sleeping.*

Q **How does that play out? Meaning that parents demand too much of the baby such as going from errand to errand?**

A *Exactly. That they don't make enough time in the day for the baby to sleep; they haven't budgeted that in appropriately.*

Q **What do you make of the idea that some babies are "good sleepers" and some are not?**

A *There are some babies who are naturally good sleepers and parents can pretty much do anything and the baby will do fine. Then there are other babies who are high-strung or anxious or whatever we want to call them and even under the best management they are difficult to get to sleep well. A big mistake parents often make is to cave in right away and say, "Oh, my baby is not a good sleeper" when they really haven't tried all the right things.*

Q **Right. Actually when I was reading Dr. Ferber's book it said to try to avoid jumping to the conclusion that your child is a poor sleeper because it actually ends up**

influencing your own behavior.

A Exactly. But I would also say a well-slept baby is a good baby. The better they sleep, the happier they are. It's a work in progress and parents need to just continue looking for the right answers.

Q If a parent came into your office and said "my child is not sleeping through the night, he's six months old, and I am not comfortable listening to crying," what advice would you give her?

A I would start by exploring with her why she was uncomfortable with the crying. In other words, what were the parents worried was going to be the problem? Did they think the child was going to feel unwanted? And I would tell them I didn't think that was the case. Did they think it was physically bad for the child? And I would tell them I didn't think that was the case and I would try to explore what their feelings were and maybe we could come to some compromise to help them deal with the crying. Because at some point, whether it's about sleep or a discipline issue, they're very likely to face a situation where they're going to have to say no.

Once I got through that stage I would say let's explore the other things that you are doing that are counterproductive to sleep. That's why I wrote the book [Is My Child Overtired?]. My book is aimed to start pre-birth—to begin thinking about sleep—and then immediately after birth to focus on sleep habits. You know, everybody wants to focus on the crying-it-out thing but my feeling is, if you do all these other things that are sleep enhancing you're not going to have to deal much with the crying it out. I'm not going to guarantee you won't have some crying but if you do all these other things like not letting the child get overtired and not letting them sleep in more than one place, any crying it out will be minimal compared with starting with the notion at four months that you're going to have to let a child cry it out.

Q Another question I have about crying is how parents can learn to discern hunger cries from other cries. And at what age does this really become a possibility?

It can be as early as a couple of weeks, believe it or not. In some circumstances you can do that but you have to start with the premise that the baby is healthy and is gaining weight consistently. And then you just see what happens. If your child was fed, slept for an hour and a half—and here we're talking a three-week-old—wakes up crying and you put the baby to breast and she sucks for a minute or two and goes back to sleep again, you misread that. So it's not just the sound of the cry, which I think people tend to focus on, but it's more the circumstances as well. When did they last feed? How much or how long did they take at the feeding? Have they been up too long? Are they just downright overtired?

That's helpful—that it's not just the sound but the circumstance because the way this is talked about in books it implies it's a sound you're listening for.

Right.

Okay, if you are trying different sleep approaches, how long before you decide something is working or not working?

I would say about a week. Usually, things are better in three or four days if you're on the right track. Usually what happens is people have left out important segments of the plan such as they're allowing the child to sleep in several different places or keeping the child up too long, that sort of thing.

Well, it would be easy to do because there's so much to think about.

Is there an effective way and a less effective way to use a pacifier for naps and at night?

I don't know if I would word it as an effective and not effective way—I think there's a good and a bad way. You shouldn't use a pacifier in a breastfed baby until you know

Ch. 4

you've got the breast-feeding established—in other words, until you know the baby's gaining weight, latch is good, everything's on track. That could be as early as two weeks but it could be a month. That's an important proviso about pacifiers.

My philosophy on pacifiers is you make it part of the child's bed. You can have a pacifier any time but you have to be in your bed to have it. Acknowledge that it is merely a sleep aid, and if you want your pacifier, that means you're tired and the place we want you when you're tired is in your bed.

Okay, and what if you're dealing with a three-month-old who always spits the pacifier out during the night and wakes up crying? Do you get up to put it back in the child's mouth?

You go on to plan B. You give it up and say this isn't working for us, find your thumb or a position or something.

If a baby is waking several times at night and in the wee morning hours, what do you feel is a reasonable time to call off attempts to sleep and begin the day?

It depends where you live and what your work is, but usually I tell parents at 6:00 A.M., just start your day. Start your day early. Have that be your quality time.

Great. Is there an age when you think all babies should be sleeping through the night and does it differ for breast-and bottle-fed babies?

Yes, it certainly does for breast and bottle. There are no hard and fast rules but an eight- or nine-month-old breastfed baby who is still waking once at night, if that's a good solid feeding, there's nothing wrong there—that's just the cost of doing business. It doesn't mean that all eight- or nine-month old breastfed babies are doing that but it happens in many cases. From the standpoint of a bottlefed baby, I think that baby should be able to achieve sleeping through by six months.

Those are nice, generous time-frames, because a lot of the books out there actually say three or four months. Now I know that you're not a believer but if there is co-sleeping going on, is there an optimal age to transition a child to a crib or bed?

Now let me go back and clarify my co-sleeping position. One thing that is pretty clear is that babies that have good access to their moms start to gain weight better if they're breast-feeding and I think if there's an argument for co-sleeping or modified co-sleeping it's in that first month of life when you're really trying to get breast-feeding going.

So you could either have your baby in bed or in a bassinet nearby?

Right. With co-sleeping, there are gradations and it's not all or nothing.

As most books tell us, napping at home is optimal, but what if your schedule cannot accommodate naps at the same time every day in a crib due to picking up older siblings or other obligations?

Again, this is not a black and white issue. This comes up a lot. Let's say you've got a three-year-old and a brand-new baby. What I tell parents is as long as that baby is going with the flow, you can do what you want to. If you have a baby who can grab sleep wherever it happens, if you can honestly describe your little baby as being happy and contented almost all the time, then you have a reasonable compromise. But if somebody has described your baby as colicky or if you cannot describe your baby as happy and contented, then you have to start doing something differently. Make sure the little baby isn't paying the biggest price.

Dr. Wilkoff lives and practices in Brunswick, ME. He is the author of *Coping with a Picky Eater, Is My Child Overtired?: The Sleep Solution for Raising Happier, Healthier Children, The Maternity Leave Breast-feeding Plan: How to Nurse Your Baby for 3 Months and Go Back to Work Guilt Free*, Fireside, 2002, and *How to Say No to Your Toddler: Creating a Safe, Rational, and Effective Discipline Program for Your 9-Month to3-Year Old*

Ch. 4

Chapter 5:
Celebrations

Showers

Showers are usually given by family members, close friends, or coworkers—typically before the baby is born. But truth be told, you'll probably still be writing thank-you notes after baby arrives! Although etiquette books will advise against a shower hosted by a family member (seen by some as the family trying to stockpile gifts for the new baby), most people feel it's perfectly fine for a relative to host a shower. Showers are, after all, a celebration of a mother and her baby on the way and are not merely about acquiring gifts.

When someone offers to host a shower for you, begin by asking how many guests she envisions hosting so that you can create an appropriate list. There is also the question of whether you want to have only women attend your party or whether you want to include the menfolk. Co-ed showers are gaining in popularity and are sometimes held at less traditional times, such as the early-evening cocktail hour.

Once you know roughly how many people to invite, create a list with names and addresses for your hostess. If she's planning to send electronic invitations using a site such as Evite, supply her with email addresses. If your shower is small and very informal, your hostess may just want to call around with the date and time. She'll let you know what she needs and you can use the guest-list worksheet in this book to compile the contact information.

Most people attending a shower expect to bring a gift. You can leave the gift selection up to guests or you can register for gifts. Registering is often important for a first baby because your wish list may be long and some of the gear is essential. Registries increase your chances of receiving those essential items and help avoid the inconvenience of receiving and returning duplicate gifts. Your guests will generally ask your hostess where you are registered and it is also perfectly acceptable for her to make this known in the invitation.

Ch.
5

Planning a Welcoming Ceremony

Depending on your culture and traditions, you may want to plan a ceremony and reception for your baby. These rites can be religious or secular, formal or informal, large or small gatherings. For some occasions, such as a baptism, it is customary to send invitations while for others, such as a bris or brit milah, family and friends are usually notified about the event and not technically "invited." Some ceremonies or celebrations may include just immediate family.

Your beliefs and the associated customs will dictate how much typical party planning you engage in for this celebration. The tools in this section are to help you plan a guest or contact list and record the gifts your baby receives. Use the available space to fit your own needs and make the event what you would like it to be.

If you are unsure about what kind of celebration you would like to have but you want to honor your baby's arrival in some way, here are some steps to take:

- Decide if your event will be religious or secular.
- Choose a location: a church, a restaurant, an outdoor spot, your home, etc.

- Decide how large or small your gathering will be.
- Determine if you have the budget for entertainment at a reception and if so, what kind would be appropriate (music, etc.)
- Try to plan a simple party. Having a new baby is a very tiring time and in this case, the spirit of the celebration—welcoming the new baby—is much more important than having the perfect hors d'oeuvres or booking the best chamber quartet in town.

Invitations and Birth Announcements

In this wonderful modern age, you have options when it comes to spreading the word about your baby's arrival. The least expensive ways to go about this is to create your own invitations or announcements if you're crafty or send word electronically. Another option, moderately expensive, is to buy pre-packaged cards that you either fill

Thank Yous

You'll be feeling plenty grateful as loved ones send a steady stream of gifts your way, and even if it takes you a few months to catch up, writing thank you notes is doable over time. Family and close friends will probably give you multiple gifts: a shower gift and then an additional present when your baby is born. If you plan a welcoming ceremony, either religious or secular, your baby will receive more gifts on this occasion. A gift is not always material but may come in the form of a favor: an errand run, a meal cooked, childcare for an older child, all deeds worthy of a note. It is appropriate to thank someone for each gift or favor, even if you end up writing three or four notes to the same person. When you venture to the stationery store, buy in bulk.

Ch.
5

in by hand or run through your laser printer at home. And then there are custom announcements—either photo, stationery, or a combination.

You can find affordable solutions, even in the custom world, by creating announcements using an online photo store such as Kodak Gallery, Shutterfly, or Snapfish. The cost is about one-third the price of custom stationery. If cost is a barrier to sending birth announcements at all, consider using a site like www.sendomatic.com. For under $15 you can send electronic invitations or announcements to up to a 100 people. This method also saves you the expense of postage.

You can use the space below to write down ideas or information about locations, officiants, entertainers, and their availability

Notes:_____

_____

_____

_____

_____

_____

_____

_____

_____

_____

_____

_____

Ch.
5

Custom Birth Announcements

Custom announcements are expensive. The upside is that they are a unique keepsake and you have a world of options when creating them. You may want to spend some time in your favorite stationery store looking through options and samples. Once you do, you'll recall the stationery jargon you first heard when planning your wedding. Just in case, here's a little refresher:

- **Decide if your event will be religious or secular.**

- **You can choose both the stock—the thickness of the paper your announcement is printed on—and the color of the announcement.** Announcements often have a light background color, showcasing your words and a cute design or motif.

- **Motif or design:** Different stationery companies offer an array of motifs for announcements such as ducks, stars, bunnies, etc. Motifs can be printed with ink, embossed, or debossed. Borders are another design option. Then there are accessories such as decorative ribbons, vellum, and more.

- **Ink color:** Once you choose your wording, you'll need to select an ink color.

- **Printing method:** Thermography or engraving. Thermography is less expensive than engraving. Engraving is considered more formal than thermography.

- **Photo:** Some announcements accommodate a photo, others do not.

- **Ordering envelopes in advance:** very convenient because you can address them before your baby is born in the weeks when you are not feeling so active yet do not have a little one to tend to. This can be tough if you don't know the sex of your baby, though, because it requires choosing an announcement before your baby is born. You can always choose unisex colors.

Ch 5

Stationery store or website: _____

Wording: _____

_____

_____

_____

Date ordered: _____ Date expected: _____

Notes: _____

_____

_____

_____

Don't forget to send word of your baby's arrival— and possibly a photo—to publications such as your school's alumni magazine or a local newspaper.

Resources:

Electronic:

www.evite.com

www.its-party-time.com

www.sendomatic.com

Stationery:

www.invitingsmiles.com

www.finestationery.com

www.paperstyle.com

www.peapod-announcements.com

www.picturemeperfect.com

www.polkadotdesigns.com

Photo announcements

www.kodakgallery.com

www.shutterfly.com

www.snapfish.com

Novelty (candy bars)

www.wrappedhersheys.com

Guest List

(for shower or welcoming ceremony)

Name	Address	Email or Phone	RSVP Y/N

Ch. 5

Ch.
5

Name	Address	Email or Phone	RSVP Y/N

Gift Log

Record any gifts you recieve prior to your baby's birth in the "shower gift" column and use the "welcome gift" column to record any gifts received after the birth of your baby. Use the column in the far right to track the mailing of birth announcements. The idea is to make life easy by only having to track down each person's name and contact information once.

Names and Address	Shower Gift	Thanks	Welcome Gift	Thanks	Announce-ment

Ch. 5

Find this worksheet online at www.babyfilebook.com

Tip: hand your planner over to a friend attending your shower so that she can record the names and gift descriptions for you right in this book. It will save you transferring your thank you list later on.

Names and Address	Shower Gift	Thanks	Welcome Gift	Thanks	Announce-ment

Ch. 5

Names and Address	Shower Gift	Thanks	Welcome Gift	Thanks	Announce-ment

Ch.
5

Part 3
Looking Ahead

Chapter 6:
Childcare

As you look ahead and think about returning to work, you'll have to weigh some options and decide on the childcare scenario that will best suit your family. For many families, there is little choice in the matter: in-home care is much more expensive than daycare and often finances dictate what is possible. Whether you have the luxury of hiring a nanny to care for your child at home or whether you plan to find a daycare center for your baby, there are still some options within each of these categories. This section explores some of the advantages of each type of care and will help guide you through the process of finding childcare.

What is optimal childcare? It's simple: any scenario that brings you peace of mind while you're away from your baby. If you can go to work knowing that your baby is safe, nurtured and stimulated, while you can spend your day relatively free of worry, then you have found the right childcare solution.

Nanny vs. Daycare

Below is a brief overview of some advantages and disadvantages
to hiring a nanny vs. choosing daycare.

	In-home Care (Nanny/Au pair)	Daycare
Attention	Individualized attention for your child	Less individualized attention than in-home care
Care Continuity	Even if child is sick, someone is on-hand to care for him/her	Sick children must stay home, so must you
Care Dependence	Dependent on one person, if your nanny cannot come to work, you need plan "B"	Not relying on sole caregiver, care always available
Cost	More expensive than daycare	More affordable than in-home care
Health	Child less likely to get sick (less contact with other children)	Infants likely to get sick more frequently from contact with other children
Socialization	Fewer opportunities to interact with other children	Substantial interaction with other children

Ch.
6

Daycare Centers

You have two basic options when it comes to care outside your home: a daycare center or a family daycare provider. Daycare centers can seem similar at first blush: you may read brochures describing similar philosophies (learning through play and developmental approaches are popular right now), caregiver to child ratios may be similar from center to center, and even daily routines and activities may sound more or less the

....

Never visit a daycare during scheduled naptime. You want to visit when the room will be full of active children—preferably in the afternoon when children and caregivers alike will not be fresh as morning daisies.

....

Ch. 6

same. There is nothing like visiting programs to distinguish one from another. As you make the rounds and do some on-site comparisons, you'll find that the physical environments and the cultures of each program can be quite different. It's not uncommon to have a gut feeling about a program almost as soon as you walk through the door. In this chapter you will find a worksheet with criteria to help you evaluate different daycare centers. Although the points listed on the worksheet are important, do not neglect what your instincts are telling you.

Meeting the director and several caregivers will definitely help you along in your choice as well. Instead of primarily counting on a thorough checklist, talk with the caregivers, observe them in action, and try to come away with an impression of the people who are the heart of any program. All the newest, shiniest, educational toys in the world cannot make up for people who are less than enthusiastic or stretched too thin.

Ideally, you should see caregivers making eye contact with children, looking reasonably relaxed, and making an effort to respond to individual needs as quickly as possible. Listen to what the caregivers are saying to babies and toddlers. Is there a warm and respectful tone in the room? An hour's observation will usually give you more information than a wordy description of a program's philosophy.

Either during your visits or as follow-up, make sure to gather information about the following: The ratio of caregivers to children is important in evaluating a center. "Class" size, or how many children are in one room, is also a consideration. You may want to

What does it mean when a daycare facility is licensed?

Most childcare centers are licensed by the Department of Social Services or a similar state-level department. Licensing ensures that a facility meets a minimal standard for health and safety protection. Licensing does not, however, guarantee the quality of a day care center. Many important elements of quality childcare—such as staff training, curriculum, or parent participation—are outside the purview of licensing. All licensed centers are not created equal so visit, observe, and ask questions.

A license is an essential requirement, but some centers go a step further and seek accreditation, often from the National Association for the Education of Young Children (NAEYC). While accreditation is important and reassures parents that a facility meets certain educational, health, and safety standards, you may not want to rule centers out if they are not yet accredited. Many daycare providers find that the process of applying for accreditation is time consuming and costly and it is burdensome when resources could be allocated elsewhere. Besides, in the U.S. overall, fewer than 10 percent of daycare centers are currently accredited, so you may find many high-quality settings that lack this official stamp of approval.

Ch. 6

obtain this information early on to decide if a particular program is worth a visit. In most states, requirements are particularly stringent about the care of infants. Licensing requirements vary by state but as a general rule, there should be no more than four infants or toddlers under the care of each adult. In larger centers, there should be a separate room for infants with a team of dedicated caregivers. Infants and toddlers are generally not in the same space for safety reasons.

Ask about the background and training of the director and staff members. Directors tend to have a wide range of experience, many with bachelors or advanced degrees. Staff should have, at a minimum, a year of training in the field of child development or early childhood education. The majority of daycare caregivers do not hold bachelors degrees.

Inquire about staff turnover. Ask how long each caregiver in the infant room, for example, has been with the center. Ask for an average length of stay as well. Turnover is important: it tells you something about employee satisfaction and the likelihood that your baby will receive care from one person for an extended time period. In general, staff attrition in daycare centers is very high.

There are a few steps to beginning a daycare search and some basic guidelines to keep in mind:

1. Plan ahead! Quality, affordable daycare is in great demand and spaces fill up quickly.

You may want to begin searching at the end of your first trimester. This sounds completely crazy but many centers have long wait lists and if you plan to return to work when your baby is roughly three months old, you may need this much lead time.

2. Obtain a list of licensed daycare and/or family daycare providers in your state. This can often be accomplished through an online search. The best site to begin with is www.childcareaware.org. Here you can search by zip code for a local childcare referral agency which will be able to provide a list of licensed centers in your community and possibly offer you some information about specific centers. Usually there is no fee for this valuable service.

3. Some daycare centers offer priority enrollment to employees of certain companies or members of particular congregations so this is a good time to inquire about affiliations.

4. Call programs in your area for general information: enrollment (how many children are at the center and what is the age range), fees, space availability, and hours of operation.

5. Decide on a few centers to visit and schedule tours/meetings.

6. Once you visit a program and determine it is in the running, ask for references and follow through. Other parents will give you a fair and honest assessment of their experience. Try to ask specific questions: instead of "Did you like the daycare?" try "Can you tell me about two or three things you liked best about the daycare." If references do not give glowing reports, you can ask them for other suggestions in your community.

Many family daycare providers are not licensed but operate regardless. If they are not licensed, it means that they either do not meet state standards for safety and health or they do not meet educational requirements for childcare providers in your state. You can confirm the status of a family daycare provider by requesting a list of licensed family providers from your state childcare agency.

Family Daycare

A family childcare provider cares for several children (the number is limited by state licensing requirements), and sometimes this group includes the caregiver's children. Family daycare is often a very attractive option because you are choosing a licensed facility but it is in someone's home and therefore not at all institutional. Your child receives all the benefits of a group setting but the group is small enough that the atmosphere will not be overwhelming, as some larger centers can be.

Ch. 6

If you are leaning toward choosing a family daycare provider, it is even more important to plan ahead because often these settings can only accommodate four or five children total with no more than two infants. These settings can be optimal, but it can be harder to find space available, especially for infants.

In-Home Care: The Nanny

Hiring someone to care for your baby at home can be a very attractive option. For many parents, especially when returning to work part or full-time while an infant is very young, there is an increased sense of security in knowing that the baby will be in the comfort of your own home with a dedicated caregiver. In some cases, families find they have no choice but to hire someone to come into their home. This can be because of schedule (having to be at work by 6:00 A.M. three days a week),

If hiring a nanny is prohibitively expensive, consider "share-care." This means finding a friend, neighbor, or coworker with a child similar in age who would like to share a caregiver. You can then decide in which house the children will be cared for and split costs.

because you only need part-time care, or because there are few slots available for infants in many centers.

There are very few drawbacks to choosing in-home care. The most notable obstacle is cost: hiring a nanny can be at least twice as expensive as daycare. Depending on where you live, hourly rates will vary, but in major cities, nannies often charge between $12–$18 per hour. Once you decide how many hours of care you'll need per week and do some calculations, you'll know if this route is going to work for your family or if it will be too expensive.

Aside from cost, another concern is relying on a sole person to care for your child. When your nanny gets sick or has unexpected family obligations of her own, you will need a backup plan; for many parents this means missing work for a day or two. Reliability is a big factor when hiring a nanny: make sure to inquire about reliability when you talk with a nanny's references. If you have a cadre of friends and family willing to pinch-hit, then this is less of a concern.

Finally, many parents feel concerned about the safety of their baby when they walk out the door and leave someone else in charge. Unlike a daycare center where there are several people present at any time, a home caregiver has no checks and balances. This is a natural worry. However, there are ways to gain confidence about the person you've hired. Initially, you will have either received a referral or done some kind of background check and you

The good old-fashioned spot-check is a great way to alleviate fears and find out what's going on at home. This means returning home to collect something you "forgot" when you are not expected or asking a friend to pop over during the day on some pretense. You can tell a lot about your caregiver and the environment in your home if you drop in unannounced from time to time.

Ch. 6

will have checked references. In addition, although controversial, there is an entire industry built around helping you feel more secure. Buying a "nanny-cam" reassures some parents about what is going on at home when they are not present.

Nanny or Au Pair?

A nanny is a babysitter who can live in or out of your house. Many nannies are experienced childcare professionals who enjoy caring for children and have made it their life's work. Some nannies work with one family for ten years or more. A nanny typically performs childcare duties and sometimes light housework, such as picking up toys, cleaning dishes, and washing the children's clothes.

An au pair is usually a college-age student who wants to work and live abroad for a year. Au pair programs provide a year-long cultural exchange experience that is mutually beneficial for au pairs and host families. In this arrangement an au pair lives with a family and is responsible for childcare and possibly some light housework, up to about 45 hours per week. In return,

a host family provides a weekly stipend, room and board, and sometimes a nominal education stipend, which is factored into the annual cost. The cost of hiring an au pair is much less than hiring a nanny: fees average about $250 per week.

The main caveat is that au pair programs were not created as a childcare solution for American families. Your au pair may have more interest in the cultural experiences outside your walls than inside and may have only limited experience working with children. During the interview process you can get a sense of an au pair's interests and level of childcare experience. If you plan to pursue this option, you will need to contact a US government authorized agency to legally bring an au pair into the United States from abroad. *See Resources.*

Ch. 6

Finding and Hiring a Nanny, Step-by-Step

Once you have decided on in-home care, assess your needs and write a job description. (See the *Family Needs Assessment Worksheet*.)

Network like crazy. Word of mouth is a great way to find a nanny. Get the word out during your pregnancy if possible, especially if you know you will be returning to work on a specific date.

If you are hiring a nanny, begin interviewing close to the time you want her to start. For au pairs, begin working with an agency about six months prior.

- Prescreen applicants by phone.

- Create a set of interview questions and a list of job expectations.

- Interview candidates and get references. At least two references should be work references, one or more can be personal.

- Call references and conduct background checks. If you plan to conduct a back-ground check on a candidate, she will need to agree by signing a form and providing her social security number. Background checks can be done to obtain information about criminal record, motor vehicle record, credit history, and child abuse history. Each company that provides background checks will have its own release form, but see below for a link to a sample form: www.4nannies.com/forms/Background SearchRelease.pdf

- Schedule a follow-up interview or a time for the caregiver to meet your child.

- Offer the job to a candidate and agree on terms.

- Begin a trial period, usually between one and three months.

Ch. 6

The Nanny Search

There are three main ways to find a nanny: by word of mouth, by placing an ad in a newspaper or on a community bulletin board (print or online), or by working with an agency.

A referral from a friend or coworker is arguably the best way to find a nanny. Nothing is more reassuring than having someone you know say "this person is reliable, kind, and great with kids." While there is no guarantee that a perfect match for a friend's family will work for yours, you are already miles ahead of the game when you get a referral. You should network to get referrals. Don't overlook your workplace as a resource because many companies have bulletin boards for posting this kind of information.

As another option, you could post an ad describing what kind of help you need, for how many hours a week, and what level of experience you prefer. Truthfully, when I tried this (craigslist.org in the Bay area), I was swamped. I must have received a hundred responses in a day and many of the respondents were computer science students who had a cousin they took care of for a day one time. You get the idea: not a fruitful search. You may have a greater chance of success with this method if you choose targeted bulletin boards such as a place of worship or a community center.

If you have a local resource like craigslist, you can try turning this search on its head, because you'll find many families advertise for their nannies when they have to cut back hours. This happens when kids grow up and begin attending school all day or when one parent is laid off from a job.

Ch. 6

I f you have a local resource like craigslist, you can try turning this search on its head, because you'll find many families advertise for their nannies when they have to cut back hours. This is almost like a referral—except that you do not personally know the employer—and presumably any family trying to help their nanny find work is entirely pleased with her performance. This happens when kids grow up and begin attending school all day or when one parent is laid off from a job, etc.

Alternatively, many parents opt to use an agency to find a nanny. It is expensive but there are some conveniences that come with it. The main advantage is time saved. Most agencies will have pre-screened nannies by phone (ideally, in person as well), many agencies will perform background checks and verify certifications for you, and most will have some kind of replacement policy or guarantee if a nanny leaves before the end of one year. Not all agencies are created equal, so you will need to ask very specific questions about each agency's role in the placement process and their level of support following placement. Above all, know what you are getting for the fees being charged.

The Family Needs Assessment

Now that you have some ideas about the search process, you'll need to decide who you're searching for. When you begin your search for a nanny, it's easy to get caught up in a job description: what hours you expect a nanny to work, what household responsibilities you expect her to handle, etc. While job expectations are very important, there is more to the hiring process. To get the most out of your search and interviews, it's helpful to think about what kind of person you're looking for. This means considering personal qualities in a candidate, considering who you are as parents, and taking your child's personality into account.

Ch. 6

Try to imagine candidates walking through the door, one by one. What kind of person do you have in mind as an ideal? Are you looking for a wise, gentle soul with infinite patience? Are you looking for a crisp Mary Poppins type? Or, deep down, are you basing your ideal on qualities in a particular family member? You will most likely be comparing candidates to a personal ideal and it's important to get a sense of what that is beforehand.

What kind of person do you think would bond well with your child? What kind of style do you hope she'll have? Beyond personal characteristics, such as high energy or quiet and calming, how do you want a nanny to interact with your child on a daily basis? And do you want someone who takes charge or someone who asks a lot of questions and takes more direction from you? Consult the Family Needs Assessment worksheet for some help in answering these questions.

The Interview Process

There are many books that offer guidance in the search and hiring process. They provide information, lists of things to consider and interview questions you may want to ask. While this book is no exception (see the Interview Questions for In-home Care worksheet) it's important to keep a general principle in mind when you start your search: "nanny" is a catch-all term and it describes an incredible range of potential applicants. If you can, try to adjust your interview style and your questions based on who you have sitting in your living room at a given moment.

Consider this scenario: a 19-year-old student from Ivy University shows up for her interview ready to answer questions about her greatest strengths, greatest weaknesses, what she likes most about caring for children, what she likes least, and finally, sweep you off your feet by describing herself in three illuminating adjectives. Her

Ch. 6

finishing touch is a series of thoughtful questions about your child and a timely thank you letter. Perhaps you recognize this interview format.

Your next candidate is 65 years old. She grew up in Fiji but she has lived in the U.S. for more than 40 years and worked as a nanny since the day she arrived. She shows up ready to demonstrate her warmth toward your child, her competence as a caregiver, and will gleefully tell you about the children she has cared for over the years. She may or may not sing her own praises, so you might hear more about how much she enjoyed the children than vice versa.

The nanny with 40-plus years of child-care experience may calm a baby just by giving her a special pat and a wink. She probably runs rings around the college student, but you may have to alter your litany of questions to get the most out of each interview. If you hit a roadblock in an interview, see if you can get at the informa-tion you want in another way. Sometimes

> If your state requires that you have workers' compensation insurance in order to employ someone in your home, check your homeowners' insurance policy; many include workers' compensation.

anecdotal information both breaks the ice and also gives you valuable insight into someone's character in a way that the stiffer interview questions never can. Be careful not to fall prey to your own preconceived ideas of what these interviews should be: the best nanny is not necessarily the best at talking about being a nanny.

There are several ways to manage this tax obligation. There are a number of companies that provide both payroll and tax services. You can streamline your life and be 100% compliant for a service fee. Another option is to enlist the help of your accountant if you

Ch. 6

usually have your taxes prepared. Not only can your accountant offer advice on current tax rates and obligations, he or she can also assist with any withholding and quarterly or annual tax payments. As we know, accountants also charge for their services so this

The "Nanny Tax"

It's no wonder that many parents are puzzled by the "nanny tax." The government keeps trying to make this simpler, but if you consult the IRS website and find yourself befuddled and overwhelmed, you are not alone. Below are some basic guidelines about paying taxes on household employee wages. (Consult the Resources section for additional help.)

When are you off the hook for nanny taxes? You do not need to pay tax on your nanny's wages if:

- You employ a relative to care for your child
- You employ someone under 18 for whom "nannying" is not a primary occupation: a student, for example
- You pay your nanny less than $1500 annually (this figure—the IRS wage threshold—increases about every two years)

If you don't fit into any of the above categories, you owe taxes on your nanny's wages. The "nanny tax" is simply a way of referring to three federal taxes: Social Security and Medicare tax, collectively known as FICA, and Federal Unemployment tax, also called FUTA. You will also owe state taxes, which vary depending on where you live but may include state unemployment tax and state disability tax. You'll have to contact the appropriate state agency to find out what is required in your state. The IRS has a listing of state agencies on its website (see IRS Publication 926).

Ch. 6

whole nanny proposition just got more expensive! A hefty salary, taxes, and now paying someone to manage the mountain of paperwork you created in deciding to become an employer.

Don't despair. There's always the do-it-yourself option. Having access to online resources makes this doable. There are also software programs you can buy that will help you calculate and manage your tax withholding or payments. You will probably pay a small frustration tax as you set about figuring it all out, but you will ultimately save some money and may get an education in the process. The Resources section has suggestions to point you in the right direction.

Resources

Daycare

• **Childcare Resource and Referral (CCR&R):** www.childcareaware.org, 800-424-2246. The site will allow you to search by zip code (or state) for childcare referral agencies in your state that can help you verify which centers meet your state's requirements and which are likely to be a good fit for your family. No fee. A great place to start your search for daycare.

Other resources on the site include a childcare agreement useful for share care scenarios and family daycare, tips on making care by a relative work smoothly, and a comprehensive glossary of childcare terms.

• **National Childcare Information Center:** www.nccic.org, 800-616-2242. Among other useful resources, you'll find a chart with licensing regulations and child to staff ratio restrictions by state.

• **National Resource for Health and Safety in Childcare:** nrc.uchsc.edu, 800-598-KIDS. This site, run by the University of Colorado, provides detailed information about state licensing regulations.

• **Your state department of social services.** Search online for: " _____ (your state) department of social services" and you should be able to find links to a site that will generate an instant list of licensed centers by city or county.

Ch. 6

• National Association for the Education of Young Children: www.naeyc.org, 800-424-2460

• National Association for Family Childcare: www.nafcc.org, 800-359-3817.

· ·

In-home Care

• A comprehensive site and a goodplace to start: www.nannynetwork.com

• International Nanny Association: www.nanny.org, 1-888-878-1477

• To download a childcare contract: www.nolo.com. Look in the Family Law and Immigration section.

• U.S. Citizenship and Immigration Services: uscis.gov/graphics, 800-375-5283. Helpful FAQ section on employment eligibility.

· ·

Print Resources

• *The Nanny Book: The Smart Parent's Guide to Hiring, Firing, and Every Sticky Situation* in Between by Susan Carlton and Coco Myers

• *The Nanny Kit: Everything you Need to Hire the Right Nanny* by Kimberly Porrazzo

• *Making Childcare Choices: How to Find, Hire and Keep the Best Childcare for your Kids* by Gail Sagel and Lori Berke

· ·

Payroll and Tax Resources

Payroll:
There are several companies that offer payroll and payroll tax preparation services for household employers. Three are listed below:

• **The HomeWork Solutions** site features a free nanny tax calculator and has a useful FAQ section: www.4nannytaxes.com, 1-800-NANITAX

• **Nanny Tax, Inc.** offers free consultations by phone: www.nannytax.com, 888-NANNYTAX

• **Economical** payroll/tax service and user-friendly site: www.paycycle.com

Taxes:
• For clear, concise explanations about tax obligations and a tax calculator: www.smartmoney.com/tax

Ch. 6

IRS

• To download forms and publications, visit **www.irs.gov**. Start by accessing IRS Publication 926, the Household Employer's Tax Guide. You can also download Form SS-4, which you will need to obtain an Employer Identification Number (EIN) and Schedule H, Household Employment Taxes, which is filed with your federal tax return.

• You will need to order Forms W-2 and W-3 by calling 1-800-TAXFORM. You can also reach the IRS with employment tax questions at 1-800-829-4933.

. . . .

Background Checks

If you decide to conduct a background check, you may want to find an agency to perform the check in your state. For example, Trustline in California or ChildLine in Pennsylvania. If your nanny has lived and worked in more than one state, you need to request background checks in each state. Below are some companies that offer nationwide pre-employment screening services:

• **Nanny Network Background Services:** www.nannynetwork.com

• **PFC Information Services:** www.pfcinformation.com (510) 653-5061

• **Nanny Background Check:** www.nannybackgrounds.com 866-228-3967, ext. 101

• **Backgroundsonline:** www.backgroundsonline.com 800-838-4804

• **National Association of Professional Background Screeners,** a list of member agencies: www.napbs.com

. . . .

Au Pairs

Extensive resources and list of U.S. Government-approved agencies with contact information and links.

•

www.nannynetwork.com/OtherResources/aupair.cfm

• **International Au Pair Association:** www.iapa.org

Ch. 6

Contact Information and Prescreening: In-home Caregivers and Daycare Centers

When prescreening, ask questions that are deal-breakers for you.
For example, if you require prior experience working with infants, establish
this before setting up an interview. If a daycare center must open by 7:00 A.M.
to accommodate your schedule, make hours part of prescreening.

Name: _____

Referred by: _____

Phone/Email: _____

Other: _____

Interview/tour date and time: _____

Notes: _____

_____

Name: _____

Referred by: _____

Phone/Email: _____

Other: _____

Interview/tour date and time: _____

Notes: _____

_____

Ch.
6

Name: _____

Referred by: _____

Phone/Email: _____

Other: _____

Interview/tour date and time: _____

Notes: _____

. . . .

Name: _____

Referred by: _____

Phone/Email: _____

Other: _____

Interview/tour date and time: _____

Notes: _____

. . . .

Ch.
6

Name: _____

Referred by: _____

Phone/Email: _____

Other: _____

Interview/tour date and time: _____

Notes: _____

Name: _____

Referred by: _____

Phone/Email: _____

Other: _____

Interview/tour date and time: _____

Notes: _____

Name: _____

Referred by: _____

Phone/Email: _____

Other: _____

Interview/tour date and time: _____

Notes: _____

Name: _____

Referred by: _____

Phone/Email: _____

Other: _____

Interview/tour date and time: _____

Notes: _____

Ch.
6

Daycare Evaluation Sheet

Suggestions for using this worksheet: Write the name of each center (or an abbreviated name) in the top row for your reference. Some of the questions below have yes/no answers. Where this is not the case, consider rating criteria for each center on a scale of 1 to 5 with 1 being worst and 5 being best or use another rating system that will be useful to you when you go over your notes.

General Considerations:				
Is the daycare center licensed? Accredited*?				
Is the location convenient to your home or work?				
Are the center hours compatible with your schedule(s)?				
Program Approach/ Structure:				
Do you agree with the program philosophy?				
Make note of one or two words that highlight the approach at each program. (For example: "nurturing" or "play-based")				
Does each child have a consistent caregiver or group of caregivers?				
What is the caregiver to child ratio?				
Ask about staff turnover rates. Do most teachers return each year?				
Does the center have a consistent daily routine?				

Ch.
6

Ch.
6

Program Approach/Structure:			
How much time do children spend outdoors each day?			
What is the program's philosophy on discipline?			
Do you see evidence of limit-setting?			
How skilled are caregivers at resolving conflicts between children? What is the main strategy?			
Is parent participation in the program encouraged?			
Does the center have a way of communicating with parents and giving feedback about a child's development? (Daily logs, conferences, etc.)			
What are the visitation policies? Consider it a red flag if a center requires you to call before visiting.			
What is the policy for late pick-up? It is not uncommon for centers to charge $5 or $10 per minute that you are late.			

Program Observations:				
Are babies and children content overall and engaged in interesting activities?				
Is the center a pleasant place to be? Is there natural light in the room?				
Does the atmosphere in the room seem reasonably controlled? Children make noise but you should not witness total chaos.				
Observe the relationship between babies and caregivers. Look for responsiveness, enthusiasm, eye contact, etc.				
When you ask about the other babies, do the caregivers seem to know a lot about each child's personality and needs?				
Do infants spend time moving around freely and being held? Or are they mostly in swings or cribs during the day?				
Do you see quality, age-appropriate toys and books available for children?				
Is the director open to your questions and responsive to your concerns?				

Ch. 6

Cleanliness:				
Is the overall appearance of the facility clean?				
Is the center profession-ally cleaned? How often?				
Are all surfaces, (especially floors for crawlers), kept clean?				
Is there a sink nearby so that staff can wash hands frequently throughout the day (especially after diapers are changed)?				
You should not smell any strong odors (urine, etc.) unless you are right next to the changing area.				
Safety:				
What kind of security is in place? Is it satisfactory?				
Does the center require that anyone picking up your child be on a "pick up list"?				
Are indoor and outdoor play spaces free from obvious hazards and dangers? Give the center a score on child-proofing.				

Ch.
6

Safety:			
Are outdoor play spaces enclosed by tall fences?			
Based on the configuration of the space, can staff easily supervise all areas?			
Is the staff CPR and First Aid certified?			
Before hiring, does the center do background checks on staff?			
Does the center have a plan for emergencies?			
You can request access to the center's safety record (accident history) if you like as well as the Department of Health inspection record.			
Health/Nutrition:			
Will the center feed an infant breast milk instead of formula?			
If so, where will the milk be stored?			
How often are diapers changed?			
How does the program record info about feeding and diaper changes?			
Are nutritious foods offered throughout the day?			

Ch.
6

Health/Nutrition:				
What are the policies about sick children? When is a child sent home or considered too sick to come to daycare?				
Costs:				
Compare monthly or annual fees.				
Application Procedure:				
Deposit or application fee required?				
Is there a wait list? If so, how long?				
What are the possible start dates? (Sept. only, rolling)				
Space available now?				
Overall:				
Can you imagine your baby spending each day here?				
What is your gut feeling about the program?				

Ch.
6

Family Needs Assessment: In-home Care

You can use this worksheet to develop a sense of who you are looking to hire. If you decide to post an ad in a newspaper or work with an agency, this information will assist you in the process.

I Job Description

Number of hours/days per week: _____

Degree of flexibility you require in schedule: _____

Live in or live out: _____

How much prior experience is ideal: _____

Driver's license/own car: _____

Household responsibilities: _____

_____

Other responsibilities: _____

_____

Degree of English fluency required: _____

Legal status (immigration): _____

Salary/Benefits: _____

_____

Ch.
6

II Characteristics and Personal Style

List qualities of an ideal candidate. For example: patient, calm, reliable, warm, caring, respectful, high-energy, creative, independent, responsible, positive attitude, quiet, takes initiative, nurturing, fun-loving, etc.

_____

_____

_____

III Values

Beliefs about sleep: Location, use of sleep aids, "crying it out": _____

_____

Degree of interaction with baby. What do you hope a typical day would be like? _____

_____

Schedule/routine vs. less-scheduled day: _____

_____

Discipline and limit-setting: _____

_____

Religious/spiritual beliefs and considerations: _____

_____

Other: _____

_____

Ch. 6

IV Your Child

Describe your child's personality and any special needs or consideration. Does the caregiver or facility need special training of any kind?

_____

_____

_____

_____

_____

V Notes

_____

_____

_____

_____

_____

_____

_____

_____

_____

Ch.
6

Interview Questions for In-home Caregiver

The following are suggested questions to ask during an in-person interview. Add to this list and customize the questions for your situation and needs.

Contact Information and Other Essentials

Ask the candidate to write her contact information on a separate sheet of paper at the end of the interview. It is hardly welcoming to ask for someone's Social Security Number as you greet them and begin a conversation.

Name: _____

Address: _____

_____

Phone number: _____

Date of birth: _____   **Place of birth:** _____

Social Security number: _____

Driver's license number: _____   **State:** _____

Expires: _____

Ch. 1

Experience

How many years have you worked with children? _____

How many families have you worked with and for what length of time? _____

_____

What were the ages of the children you cared for? _____

_____

Describe your last position: the family, your responsibilities, etc. _____

_____

_____

Why did you leave your last position? _____

_____

What about a past work experience have you especially enjoyed or found challenging?

_____

_____

Ch.
6

Background and Training

Do you have a family of your own? How old are your children? _____

_____

When did you come to the U.S.? Do you plan to remain here? _____

Are you a U.S. citizen or legally authorized to work in the U.S.? _____

Do you plan to work as a nanny long-term? _____

Why do you enjoy taking care of children? _____

_____

Describe your educational background. Do you have any training in early childhood

education or a related field? _____

_____

_____

Have you been certified in CPR and/or First Aid in the past year? _____

_____

The Job

Tell the candidate about the position: schedule and responsibilities. Possibly reserve a discussion about compensation for later in the interview. Find out if there are any schedule conflicts.

Tell the candidate about any concerns you have, such as keeping your baby on a schedule, special dietary issues your child has, or important family values and how they may impact her work. Assess how well the candidate will match your family or to what extent she is willing to implement your plans and take your concerns into account.

Ask the candidate what kind of work environment she is looking for. What kind of expectations does she have about the job? _____

Ch. 1

_____

_____

If there are any glaring issues after discussing the job, politely end the interview at this

point. If not, and a candidate is promising, continue to cover additional topics.

Nitty Gritty

Do you smoke? _____

Do you have any health concerns or an illness that could affect your work? _____

_____

How will you get to work and return home? _____

Do you have a driver's license? If so, how long have you had one? Do you have a good

driving record? You may want to ask for a copy of a candidate's record. _____

_____

The Big Picture

Describe your ideal scenario. What would the family be like? The parents? The children?

_____

_____

Ch.
6

_____

_____

What makes a job optimal for you?_____

_____

_____

Describe the communication style between you and your employers in your most recent position. Was it comfortable for you? Why or why not? _____

_____

_____

Did you ever have a disagreement or misunderstanding with your employer? What was it and how was it resolved? _____

_____

How do you view your role as a nanny? _____

_____

What do you like to do with children? What would you do in a typical day with my baby?

_____

_____

_____

Ch.
6

Wrap-Up

It is a matter of personal preference when to begin discussing salary and benefits. If possible, get a sense of what the candidate is expecting. You can describe the compensation now or wait until you make an offer. Be prepared for some negotiation at the offer stage.

Ask if she is currently interviewing with other families. Ask when she is available to start work. _____

Discuss taking a CPR/first aid class (at employer's expense) prior to start date.

Ask for permission to conduct any background checks you plan to perform and obtain signature._____

Request references (three at a minimum).

_____

_____

_____

If you will require candidates to take a physical exam (at your expense), ask if she is willing. (Possible tests/vaccinations: TB, Hepatitus B and C) _____

Give the candidate an opportunity to ask any remaining questions. _____

_____

_____

_____

Ch.
6

End the interview. At this point you can do one of several things:

• Introduce a promising nanny to your baby (if you haven't already).

• Give the nanny a tour of your home.

• Describe what the next steps will be, such as calling references, doing a background check, trial time with baby, etc.

After the interview, take some notes right away to record your thoughts. Remember, your gut feeling about a person is as important as any of the factual questions you asked.

Ch.
6

Nanny or Au Pair Reference Sheet

When you call a reference, be sure to write down the reference's and candidate's name so you can recall who goes with whom. When speaking with each reference, consider covering the following topics:

Dates of employment _____

Reason for leaving _____

How much notice was given _____

Ages of children during employment _____

Childcare duties _____

Household duties _____

Describe job performance _____

What are candidate's strengths? _____

What, if anything, could have been changed or improved? _____

Describe candidate's communication style _____

Was candidate reliable? _____

Ch. 6

How often did candidate call in sick? _____

Did you conduct any background checks? _____

Did candidate do any driving for your family? Did you supply a car? _____

Are you willing to discuss the salary and benefits you offered? _____

Overall, do you recommend him/her? _____

_____

Notes: _____

_____

_____

_____

_____

_____

_____

_____

_____

Ch.
6

Caregiver's Daily Diary

This daily record is a way to keep track of how your baby is feeling, how he's eating, and other important developments while you're away. It's designed for babies under one year who are drinking milk or formula from a bottle and beginning to eat some solid foods. You can reproduce this sheet or design one of your own.

Child's name: _____

Date: _____

Meals and Snacks

Bottles

Ch. 6

Time		Ounces	Notes
	AM/PM		
	AM/PM		
	AM/PM		
	AM/PM		
	AM/PM		
	AM/PM		
	AM/PM		
	AM/PM		
	AM/PM		
	AM/PM		

Find this worksheet online at www.babyfilebook.com

Solids

Time	Food(s) eaten	Notes (ate well, not too fond of peas, etc.)
AM/PM		
AM/PM		
AM/PM		
AM/PM		
AM/PM		
AM/PM		
AM/PM		
AM/PM		
AM/PM		
AM/PM		

Naps

Went to sleep	Woke up	Notes (fell asleep without pacifier, etc.)
AM/PM	AM/PM	
AM/PM	AM/PM	
AM/PM	AM/PM	
AM/PM	AM/PM	
AM/PM	AM/PM	
AM/PM	AM/PM	
AM/PM	AM/PM	
AM/PM	AM/PM	
AM/PM	AM/PM	
AM/PM	AM/PM	

Ch.
6

Diaper Changes

Time changed	Contents	Notes
AM/PM		
AM/PM		
AM/PM		
AM/PM		
AM/PM		
AM/PM		
AM/PM		
AM/PM		
AM/PM		
AM/PM		

Activities and new skills: _____

_____

_____

Concerns or questions: _____

_____

_____

Supplies needed: _____

_____

_____

Ch.
6

Ask an Expert

Carrie White is a mom who chose daycare.
Carrie lives in Hopkinton, MA with her husband, Jon, and two daughters.

When you started thinking about childcare, did you know you wanted to put your daughter in daycare or did you have other options?

I did have a family option for one or two days but I pretty much knew I wanted her in daycare four or five days a week due to the socialization factor. I also knew I wanted her in a facility and not in one-on-one care because of things that can happen like baby shaking. I liked the idea of a lot of people being around.

Also, my sister had put her son in daycare and I had seen great results with my nephew.

How old was your daughter when she started daycare?

Five months. I kept her with me until I felt she was big enough to go.

When you started your search, did you begin by getting a list of licensed centers?

My husband did that by researching online. He got a list of every licensed center in our area and then we called several. We ruled some out right away based on hours and some never got back to us regarding a tour and I thought, if they can't get back to me about a tour, what if I needed to communicate with them about my child? I'm not going to hound people; they're either going to offer good customer service or they're not.

Right. Once you narrowed it down and started looking at daycare centers, what

Ch.
6

were the factors that you considered?

A The most important things were location and hours: it had to be close for both Jonathan and me, especially for him because two to three days per week he wanted to pick her up, so it needed to be near enough to the train station that he could get there in time. And of course some centers close by 5:30 and we needed one that stayed open until at least 6:00 so Jonathan could get there after work.

Security was another factor. Some centers have open doors and anyone can walk in and out. I wanted a facility where you either need to be buzzed in at the door or you are given a code by the center so you can unlock the door.

Something else that was important to us is some facilities serve lunch and snacks and at others you have to supply it for your child. It seems like a little thing but when you're trying to get one or more kids out the door, it's a big deal. You need to keep up with shopping and make sure you have certain food ready for the week. At centers that supply food you pay a little more but it was worth it to us for the convenience.

Q **I think anything extra like organizing and packing food is something to consider. You want to streamline as much as possible.**

A And we actually switched daycares recently because I knew I was having my second and the center where my daughter was going was 20 minutes each way from work. I thought the time involved in the round trip and dropping off two would get to be too much. The other reason to think carefully about location is that when a child is sick, you get a call and have only an hour to pick her up. I think it's important to be within 10 minutes of your children if you can.

Q **That can be really hard if you have a child in daycare. When your daughter is home, you're home, right?**

A Exactly. Jon and I just basically do a juggling act. I come home for half a day and

Ch.
6

then Jon comes home for half the day. We're lucky because she hasn't been really sick but I do have to say she was more susceptible to colds and ear infections in the six month to one year time. I got a lot of comments from family like "she's always sick because she goes to daycare." It was kind of a chronic runny nose. My sister-in-law's kids did not go to daycare and were never sick.

But don't you think that when kids who stay at home go to preschool they go through the same process of developing immunities?

Yes, but my family's argument was that she was too young to expose her to all those germs. Babies share toys and put them in their mouths and spread germs more than older kids. Plus babies are building up immunities during the first several months and are more susceptible than older kids. But I didn't think it was any big deal. It was the way I wanted to go, although it can be a little less convenient at first.

How many daycare centers did you visit in all?

We saw as many as we could, five or six. You can always learn something from each tour. We visited a church center that didn't have good security but I wanted to see what each one had to offer and compare them.

Ch. 6

That makes sense. When you were on the visits, was there one thing you really wanted to find out about each place?

I mostly looked at how the space was configured. In some places the rooms were too small for the number of kids and in some there were all these cribs and a very small floor area—almost no space for playing. That wasn't for me.

I think it's more of a gut feeling when you're visiting these places. You either think it's a place for you or it's not.

If you put a baby in daycare who is too young to really tell you how things are

going, what signs did you look for to reassure you it was going well?

My daughter didn't come home cranky. We asked lots of questions and also they have a daily sign-out sheet that tells you about your child's day. She was also eating and drinking a lot bottle-wise so she had no loss of appetite and I knew she was being cared for well. She was sleeping and in a good nap routine. And she was growing as an individual. You could tell that she was learning from the other children, learning to share, and I could tell she was growing from the experience.

Plus I talked to the teachers. I called during the day to check in and they would tell me how the day was going.

It sounds like they were very open and giving you a lot of feedback.

Yes, and they were always willing to give me that feedback and not act like I was breathing down their neck.

I'm sure that helps a lot. Will you choose daycare again for your younger daughter?

Yes. We already enrolled her at the center where her sister goes. There was a waiting list for the infants so we wanted to get her signed up right away.

I really like that at this center they have the infant room right next to the area where the Directors sit. Infants are more needy and I like that there are other people nearby in case the teachers need an extra pair of hands.

I think it's going to be a great place for the baby. And I'm not even five minutes away so I can go up and nurse three times a day if I want to. They can call me and ask if I want to come in for ten minutes to nurse. I prefer that to being gone for the whole day.

That sounds like the best of both worlds.

Ask an Expert

Sylvia Herrera-Alaniz is a mom who chose in-home care
Sylvia lives in Austin, TX with her husband and two children.

Tell me about your decision-making process when you were pregnant and you knew you would need childcare but you hadn't decided what kind.

I think my process was fairly easy in the sense that I had narrowed it down in my mind to two options: either at-home care—a nanny—or at someone else's home. I initially never considered a daycare center. My reason for that was that it would be more intimate and would have fewer children and hopefully therefore more one-on-one time.

So what made the decision for you?

When I went to the family daycare, I saw three or four playpens lined up against the wall and it looked like little jail cells! Just that many lined up—that one visual did it all.

I remember when I was making the decision between at-home care or family daycare I considered a few other things. One, I could afford it. Bringing someone into your home is much more expensive than bringing your child somewhere else. I was willing to pay the premium price because it saved me time (travel time to and from daycare). I spent the extra 30 to 45 minutes a day playing with my daughter. It was an investment.

Were there any other convenient aspects to in-home care?

Preparing for daycare can be time-consuming too. I think people that take babies to daycare have to prepare bottles the night before and pack changes of

Ch.
6

clothes. Then the time involved in putting the baby in the car, having to drive some-where, you lose a good 30 minutes there. During that time you could just be sitting on the floor playing so it was a matter of picking up time when I was home.

So then how did you do your nanny search?

Actually, it was networking. When you're looking for a job, when you're looking for anything, you need to cast a wide net and this is what I did. This technique was something that I learned from working. Everybody that I was acquainted with knew that I was looking for a nanny.

And how early in your pregnancy did you start looking?

Actually, not early enough. My husband was going to leave his job and we didn't know how long he was going to be out of work. He was going to be primarily taking care of the baby until he found a job so we thought about the search but we didn't actually do it until after my daughter was born when he started to job hunt.

I was home the first three months and he was home the next three months so she didn't actually go into any kind of care until she was six months old.

Once you had started networking, how many people did you actually interview?

Probably six or seven.

Oh, so you got many referrals from your networking. Then did you screen some people by phone and rule some out to decide who to interview?

No, I met all of them in person. I didn't do any phone screening.

And was everybody looking for full-time work? Was your job description really clear?

Yes, my job description was pretty well-defined. I needed a lot of flexibility

Ch. 6

because of my travel. I needed someone who was able to come in early and stay late on the days that I traveled.

I needed someone who could drive, who had their own, reliable transportation, and so there were questions about that.

And what other considerations did you have off the bat? I think I recall that some-one Spanish-speaking was important to you.

Yes, because I wanted my daughter to learn Spanish, I wanted her to hear it throughout the day. I wanted the nanny I hired to speak only Spanish to her.

So the main criteria were flexible hours, ability to drive, Spanish-speaking?

Yes. Obviously childcare experience and all the other stuff! I know, there's so much stuff. Flexibility was probably the biggest thing.

When you were interviewing nannies, did you have a set of prepared questions that you asked everybody?

Yes.

And did you feel like the questions that you asked generally elicited information that was useful? Did you rely on your questions a lot?

I relied on my questions but I also really focused on how they interacted with me and with my daughter because she attended all the interviews as well.

What kind of questions did you ask?

I asked a lot of logistical questions and also about background experience, such as "How long have you been taking care of kids?" That type of question instead of the open-ended questions. So that's why seeing the interaction with my daughter was so critical.

That makes sense. Once you interviewed people, did you rely on gut instinct to make a final choice? Was there someone who stood out for you?

I think actually I ended up offering the job to someone who couldn't take it so I went with my second choice but all of the people who came were really good and any of them would have worked.

REALLY?! I'm not sure that's a typical experience.

Well, maybe just because my network knew exactly what I was looking for.

Well, that's lucky. I interviewed six people initially and none of them worked. Once you had offered the job to someone, what kind of health screenings or background checks did you do?

Because everyone was recommended by someone I knew, I didn't do much after that. I checked to make sure she had a driver's license.

When you first walked out the door, what were the concerns you had in your mind?

What weren't the concerns? I mean, my first overnight business trip was the hardest. My concerns were more on an emotional level. Not so much "Does she know where everything is?" but will my daughter know that I'm gone, how much will she miss me, how much will I miss her, what happens if she cries for me and I'm nowhere near, I'm days away.

So it was all very emotional. Nothing to do with, will she be fed, will she be clean, nothing like that.

Ch.
6

181

Q So you didn't have concerns about the actual caregiver, that's good. At least you had total confidence in the person you hired.

A *Exactly. Probably that was because I was mostly working from a home office so I got to see what was going on day-to-day. I used to pop downstairs and check in on them all the time.*

Q Have you had any on-the-job concerns that have come up and how have you addressed them?

A *Yes, I have had on-the-job concerns. I think when anyone does any job for a length of time, there are times when they start to get lax in their work. In this case it would be they're not taking her to the park as much or doing the ABCs as often.*

I always made a comparison between this person who worked for me at home to the reps and managers who worked for me at the office and, interestingly enough, it was much easier to tell a rep or manager when something was wrong. I found that conversation very easy. However, it was extremely difficult and nerve-wracking, stressful, to even broach the subject with the person who's taking care of your child.

I always approached it and at the end of the day I took the same tack that I took as a manager. It was a conversation where we sat down and I expressed my concerns and asked them what their thoughts were. I know that when there were things going wrong in my home with my nanny I put off addressing it longer than I would have in my normal work environment.

Q I'm assuming that you feel you made the right decision in choosing a nanny. How have you seen both your daughters benefit from the one-on-one care?

A *The biggest benefit is having a sense of safety, stability and security.*

Q For you?

A *For me and for them. It was always the same person caring for them and they*

Ch. 6

had all their stuff around them on a daily basis. If it wasn't mom and dad with them, it was the nanny. I think there's a lot to be said for that—stability. In my case, there wasn't any turnover. I know that many daycare centers have high turnover.

I wish I had put older daughter into preschool sooner because she didn't go until she was three. I think preschool even earlier would have prepared her socially and academically for kindergarten because even though my nanny did really well with the Spanish, that doesn't necessarily get her ready for school.

Q Do you have any advice for parents doing this kind of search? If you had it to do over again, what would you do differently?

A *I would write down the job expectations so that everybody's really clear from the very beginning. I would treat it even more formally than I did. I would present the written expectations to them during the interview process. Things like I only want my kids to watch 30 minutes of TV per day and it has to be PBS.*

Q I think that's especially helpful, not just for the person you're hiring. If you can write a list of job expectations, it means you actually have to assess your own needs and decide what/who you're looking for.

A *Right. And things like, If it's not raining or freezing cold, the expectation is that you will spend at least an hour playing outside every day. That's the only thing I would do differently.*

Chapter 7:
Family Financial Matters

There's a saying that goes something like, "with family, comes responsibility." Right. Those of us who are getting up at 3:00 A.M. to feed infants are well acquainted with the word, "responsibility." After life has settled down a bit and you can think clearly again, you will want to delve into big-picture responsibility by creating some contingency plans for your baby and family in the event that things do not go as planned. Not only is it important to make plans and establish a safety net for your family, but it is critical to get these plans in writing.

You don't need to be a high roller to participate in what is sometimes called estate planning. The bare bones of estate planning include designating a guardian, which is usually included in a will, creating a healthcare directive (or living will), and possibly designating someone with financial power of attorney. Many parents also purchase a life insurance policy and consider buying disability insurance, additional safeguards for families.

Once you dig in, there are several scenarios to consider—all outrageously morbid—and it is best done in one fell swoop if you can manage it. Who wants to revisit these questions every few years? This section will offer some guidance about making sure your preferences are clearly stated in appropriate documents in the event of a tragedy or disabling event. The topics included in this section are:

- **Creating a will**
- **Choosing a guardian for your child**
- **Creating a healthcare directive/living will**
- **Designating financial power of attorney**
- **Purchasing life insurance and disability insurance**

Preparing a Will

Ch. 7

A Last Will and Testament serves two primary functions: it specifies who will receive your property when you die and it names a guardian for your child or children in the event that you and your spouse die before your children reach the age when they become legal adults (either 18 or 21, depending on your state). Even if all you think you have to pass on is your music collection, be sure to create a will for the sole purpose of naming a guardian. Although it is difficult to think about preparing a will, the information it contains will make the lives of those who survive you much easier. If you have a legal will, it will serve as a map to allocate your assets upon your death and smooth the process for your family.

Beyond dispensation of property and the designation of a guardian, you can also make known your wishes for funeral arrangements in your will. You can be very specific, such as including a letter stating your preferences for how you envision your children being raised and any other information you feel is relevant. Think of your will as a collection of documents to help those who survive you set plans in motion and carry out your wishes.

A will does not control the disposition of certain assets such as life insurance proceeds or retirement plans, such as IRAs, 401(k)s, pensions, or 403(b)s. It is very important to verify and/or update the beneficiary designations on file with the carrier

Wills are very personal documents expressing wishes on an array of subjects: property, guardianship, and funeral arrangements, to name a few possibilities. It follows that you will want to create a will for each parent. You will, of course, want to designate the same guardian for your child, but beyond that, the documents may or may not bear many similarities. Many spouses choose different executors and health care directives often look quite different.

or plan administrator for those items. (See the Assets worksheet for suggestions on how to keep track of this information.)

There are many reasons why it's easy to put off preparing your will, including the expense, and there are plenty of emotional obstacles, in that nobody wants to think about meeting his or her end, much less an untimely one. And then there is the question of how. Who can help with a will and how much will it really cost? It's a myth that having a will prepared is prohibitively expensive. It is possible to have a will and healthcare direc-

....

The best way to find an attorney who specializes in estate planning is to ask for referrals from friends and family. Some attorneys charge a flat fee for estate plans, which can be an advantage because you can feel free to contact them with questions—and there is no meter running. Others charge an hourly fee so you will want to know what that is and how many hours they estimate are needed to create your will.

....

tive prepared by an attorney for approximately $500. Online alternatives are even less expensive and are discussed below.

If you prefer to do things on your own, there are some excellent products on the market. Consider the Willmaker Plus Program from Quicken/Nolo, a will-writing software program. It also includes trusts, financial power of attorney, living wills, and a book on estate planning if you buy the kit option. The software has gotten rave reviews, is easy to use, and costs just $50. In addition, Willmaker will automatically create documents that reflect the laws of your state (estate plans are state-specific), removing that hurdle for you. The Nolo website (www.nolo.com) offers information about every aspect of estate planning and is full of answers for the legal document do-it-yourselfer. There are also several websites where you can download forms instead of purchasing software. Make sure that whatever forms or product you choose adheres to the laws in your state.

Ch.
7

After you create your will, you need to find a safe place to keep it. Some attorneys would counsel against keeping these documents in a safety deposit box because if your loved ones needed to access the documents, they would need a key or the assistance of a bank officer to search for the will. It's probably safer to keep them in a file cabinet at home and let one or two people know where they are.

However you decide to go about creating your will, the first thing you will want to do is create a list of your assets. Although the value of accounts and investments will change over time, you need to have a rough idea of the value of your estate so you can decide what kind of protection you need from potential estate taxes. Also—and be forewarned, I am about to venture into morbid territory again—if you or your spouse were to die, it's very handy for the survivor to have a list of where all the assets are and be able to access accounts easily. I would recommend creating this list on a computer so it can be continually updated, but you can use the worksheet in this section as a suggested format to create your list of assets.

You will want to choose an executor for your will and this applies whether you are working with an attorney or creating your own documents. An executor is the person in charge of handling your requests as stated in your will, assembling and controlling your assets, and paying any taxes that your estate may owe following your death. This person should be someone you trust and also someone good at handling finances and red tape. There is ample space in this section for notes about potential executors and people who could play other important roles.

Once prepared, wills do not need to be

A Note About Taxes

Estate taxation laws are in a continual state of flux and reform. The current federal estate tax exemption is $1,500,000 per person but the exemption will continue to grow until 2010. Estate tax exemptions are an important concern if you have a fairly large estate (the total value of your assets). Exemptions allow a certain amount of money or property to pass tax free to children, grandchildren, and other heirs. While $1,500,000 may sound like a large sum, once you factor in life insurance policy death benefits and other assets, such as real estate, you may find that your assets come closer to that mark than you may think. Also, many states impose inheritance taxes with much lower exemption amounts. If you think your assets are or will shortly be in excess of $1,500,000, you should consult an attorney to explore advanced estate planning, which may involve setting up a trust.

notarized or otherwise ratified in some official way. You do need to sign the will and any other documents in the presence of witnesses, two in most states but three in some. Neighbors or friends will do just fine. Chances are you know some other new parents who are also working on a will and you could ask friends to get together and all be witnesses for each other. If you are working with an attorney, the documents will be signed at his or her office.

Choosing a Guardian

Choosing a guardian for a child means thinking about the unthinkable and is often the biggest challenge in creating a will. That being said, it is also the most

important reason to do so. Many parents think that informing their families about who should care for their children is adequate and there is no need to be official about it. In actuality, if you die without having named a guardian, any family member or friend can offer to care for your child and a court will decide who will raise your child in your stead. Even though it is so hard to think about leaving a child in the world, it is better thought through now than ignored and it will ultimately bring you great peace of mind.

When you are thinking about who to choose as guardian, it's a good idea to work together and consider pros and cons of various arrangements. I know couples who have found this task simple: there may be a sibling who is an obvious choice, someone who presents no doubts or conflicts. In some cases, a set of grandparents on one side or the other is the perfect option. Sometimes friends of the family end up being the best alternative for any number of reasons.

For other parents, designating a guardian is arduous and difficult. Couples often disagree and the discussion can bring up uncomfortable subjects such as "I like your sister but…" If you do find yourself stuck, the first thing to acknowledge is that you will never find a guardian who is just like you. You cannot expect that your household and your life are duplicated anywhere. But with some thought, you can hopefully designate a guardian who embodies most, if not all, of the qualities you are looking for. Remind yourself that this is a back-up plan: a child has to lose both parents for this arrangement to take effect and the likelihood of that happening is very small.

Below is a list of possible considerations to help you in making your decision about a guardian.

Ch. 7

Geography, Lifestyle, and other Practical Considerations

Does the potential guardian:

- Live in another state and would relocating your child be a problem?
- Live near other important people in your child's life?
- Have other small children and have his or her hands full for the foreseeable future?

If the potential guardian:

- Does not have children of his or her own, how would raising a child fit into that person's lifestyle?
- If older, does he or she have the energy to care for a young child?

Values and Beliefs

Does the potential guardian:

- Have similar values about childrearing?
- Share your core moral values?
- Have similar religious beliefs?

- Have similar beliefs about how children should be educated?

Just when you thought you were nearing the end of this guardian business, there's one more thing: you will need to choose a back-up, or alternate, guardian in the event that the person you designate is unable or unwilling to serve as guardian at the time of your death. Also, your will is the place to designate a trustee if you choose, someone who will manage your money for your children until they turn eighteen. Sometimes the guardian and trustee are the same person. In other cases, your choice of guardian, while the best person to care for your children, may not be the best person to handle finances. Once you choose your guardian you can decide whether or not to designate a trustee in your will.

Once you make the decision about a guardian and he or she has agreed to take on the responsibility, it's time to put the plan into writing. Don't make excuses, don't wait for a good time, and don't put this off.

Ch. 7

Healthcare Directives

I'm not sure if this is good news or bad news but for most of us parents in our prime the odds of becoming medically or mentally incapacitated are higher than the odds of dying. While you are working on your will, you should think about some additional documents that address conditions short of death.

Not to be confused with a will, a Living Will is used to state your preferences for health care and life support should you become incapacitated. Beyond making your wishes known in the event of a disabling accident or illness, you will need someone to make decisions about your care when you cannot. Essentially you need two things: a document stating your preferences for care and life support and a document that gives someone else the power to act on your behalf. To empower another person to make healthcare-related decisions for you, you need what is called either "healthcare

power of attorney" or "healthcare proxy." Once you create a Living Will and designate someone with healthcare power of attorney, you have what is called a Healthcare Directive. [suggested graphic: living will + healthcare power of attorney = healthcare directive] You can also state whether or not you wish to be an organ donor and specify funeral arrangements and burial or cremation preferences as part of your Healthcare Directive.

You will need to think carefully about what you would want for care and then designate a person to help carry this out. Designate a primary healthcare proxy and an alternate to be on the safe side. Your healthcare proxy should be a tough cookie. What I mean is someone who is up to dealing with potentially stormy times among family members (just because you have stated your wishes doesn't mean everyone will agree with them) and someone who will be a strong advocate for you when dealing with the medical community and insurance companies.

Ch. 7

Again, this decision-making process is not a day at the beach, but once you have completed it you can spare your family wondering what kind of treatment—or lack thereof—you would want if you became incapacitated. Once you make these decisions and complete the forms or documents, either on your own or with an attorney, you will want to make copies and give them to your family members and especially to the person you designate as a proxy. A Healthcare Directive can be created with the help of an attorney or online by downloading forms.

Financial/Durable Power of Attorney

In the event you are mentally or physically incapacitated, you may need someone to handle your financial affairs—namely, money and property. This realm is not addressed by your Healthcare Directive (although you may choose to name the same person for both roles) so you may want to consider giving someone financial power of attorney. It's important to be sure that financial power of attorney is durable power of attorney, ensuring that it will remain effective even if you become incapacitated. You can name an agent, the term for the person you are giving financial power of attorney, as you set up your will.

Attorney Meeting Checklist

Before meeting with an attorney, here's some homework that will save you time and possibly money:

- **Compile an assets list (see page 201).**

- **Decide on an executor and an alternate choice.**

- **Decide on a guardian and an alternate choice.**

- **Decide on a trustee, if applicable.**

- **Decide on a healthcare proxy and an alternate choice.**

- **Select someone to designate with financial power of attorney and an alternate choice.**

Ch. 7

Resources

· · · · · · · · · · · ·

Wills

● **Quicken/Nolo:** www.nolo.com Will-writing software and estate planning books

● **Making a Legal Will:** *The International Last Will and Testament Directory.*
In actuality, only covers the US and UK but the site offers links to legal forms and other do-it-yourself resources: www.making-a-legal-will.com

● www.uslegalforms.com

· ·

Healthcare Directives

● **National Hospice and Palliative Care Organization:** Free healthcare directives (called "Advance Directives" on the site), state-specific forms and instructions for completing them www.caringinfo.org or call 1-800-658-8898

● The U.S. Living Will Registry electronically stores healthcare directives and makes them available to health care providers at all times. You can also access state-specific forms from this site and find links to other organizations, such as the American Bar Association.

● American Bar Association "tool kit" for health care advance planning: www.abanet.org/aging/toolkit/home.html

Ch.
7

Notes: _____

_____

_____

_____

_____

_____

_____

Life and Disability Insurance

Since we've already covered some morbid ground, I trust you won't be shocked if we delve right into life insurance. As you may already know, life insurance involves deciding how much coverage you need and then purchasing a policy, just as you do for your home or your car. This coverage is intended to help support your dependent family members in the event of your death. If you die while you are insured, your designated beneficiary— or beneficiaries—receives a death benefit in the amount of your policy. Life insurance makes sense for parents with young children for many reasons:

- **If one spouse or partner survives the other, the death benefit from the policy will replace the income the deceased spouse was earning, helping you maintain your lifestyle**

- **Death benefits help families cover immediate expenses, such as paying a mortgage, and often long-term costs as well, such as college tuition**

- **If both parents were to die simultaneously, you leave your child or children with a substantial amount of money, ensuring their needs will be met over many years and easing a potential burden on your chosen guardian**

There are two main types of life insurance: term and whole. The vast majority of families with young children opt for term insurance. Term insurance policies have a fixed term usually between 10 to 30 years, often with the option to renew. Many people find it's acceptable that the policy expires at a certain point because after children are grown, most parents do not feel the need to carry life insurance anymore. With this type of policy, if you die while insured, your family receives a death benefit. Term is quite affordable when compared to whole life insurance policies and is usually the most appropriate form of coverage for young families because annual premiums are low, making it possible to afford a

Ch. 7

greater amount of coverage.

The drawback? If you live out a long and happy life, and choose not to renew a term policy after age 60 or 65, for example, the insurance company keeps all the marbles. It sounds like you are getting the short end of the stick here but it's no different than insuring your car or your home. We do this to protect assets (in the case of cars and homes) and never expect to get anything back from insurance companies. So it is with term life: you take out a policy for a term of several years with the option to renew as needed and you actually hope to never see a dollar of this money again. It's all part of building a safety net; just like choosing a guardian, it's a contingency plan.

Whole life insurance has a dual purpose: it functions as an insurance policy and an investment account. You may have heard of universal and variable universal life insurance, both of which basically fall under the whole life insurance umbrella. The main difference between whole and term insurance

is that whole is good for the duration of your life and it steadily accrues a cash value, offering more than just a death benefit. As you pay your premiums, your account earns interest and the cash value of the account increases (theoretically) over time. Your family receives a death benefit when you die, whenever that may be. Again, there is no fixed term with this type of policy. The downside of whole life is that the premiums are substantially higher compared to term. If, however, you can afford the coverage you need and the hefty premiums that come with this coverage and you will not need the savings in your life insurance account for 10 to 15 years, it may be worth considering whole life.

Coverage: How Much Is Enough?

Once you determine what type of life insurance seems to be a fit for your family, you need to ask yourself how much

Ch. 7

Term vs. Whole Life Insurance At-a-Glance

Term Life Insurance	Whole Life Insurance
Policy expires at end of set term	Policy is good for your entire life
Premiums are generally low so you can afford to buy more coverage	Premiums are generally high so you can afford to buy less coverage
Premiums increase with age	Premiums are fixed
Simple to purchase, simple to understand. Can easily be bought over the internet or directly from company	Buying whole life is more likely to require meeting with an agent and policies are not always easy to grasp
Insures you during your working/earning years while young children depend on your income	Insures you for your entire life or policy can be cashed out during retirement years, providing income for you (and/or spouse)
You can invest money on your own that you would otherwise be spending on whole life premiums. Many other long-term investments such as IRAs have better returns than whole life policies.	Large premiums tie up money that could otherwise be invested to yield better returns.
Policy has no cash value	Policy has a cash value and offers tax-deferred savings (functions as investment account)
	Acts as a forced-savings plan. Very useful if you want to plan for retirement but are not a saver at heart.
	You can take out loans against the cash value of your policy, usually with a low interest rate, but this will decrease the death benefit until the loan is repaid.

Ch. 7

Ch. 7

There is one rather strange thing about the life insurance process. The required physical exam often takes place at your house. It turns out that there are people trained to come to our homes and draw blood while we lie around in our living rooms. It seems odd, but during this exam you can expect to answer some questions about your lifestyle and habits, have blood drawn, and have your blood pressure measured.

you need. A very simple guideline is six or seven times your annual salary. You may want to insure each parent so that if something tragic occurred, the death benefit would either replace the income that parent was earning or help your family with large expenses in the future, such as college.

Disability Insurance

Harkening back to the healthcare directive section, you may recall that we parents in our prime are more likely to become mentally or medically incapacitated than we are to die. For this reason, many parents with young children buy disability insurance. Disability insurance will replace anywhere from 45% to 60% of your income on a tax-free basis if an illness or injury prevents you from working.

Honestly, buying disability insurance is not as easy as buying term life insurance. There are as many types of policies out there as there are companies offering them. And with disability insurance, you get what you pay fo,r so the company offering the cheapest premium is not always the best choice. Unless you really enjoy reading the fine print, I would suggest meeting with an agent to purchase disability insurance if you cannot obtain it through your workplace. The price of an agent's commission will be money well spent when you get a policy that will really help you in times of trouble.

Buying Insurance

Many parents are able to purchase life and disability insurance as part of a benefits package at work. This is often relatively inexpensive (because your company subsidizes the cost) and the policy can sometimes be obtained without a physical exam. If you have this option, it's an easy route to getting insured. If you do not have a benefits package that includes life and disability insurance, you will have to do more leg work on your own, either finding an agent or buying online.

Almost anyone in the financial industry would recommend meeting with an agent to buy insurance, especially whole life insurance. Sure, the cost of an agent's commissions are built into your premiums but you are gaining valuable advice for this fee. A word of caution about the agent process: it's important that your agent is looking out for your needs first and can sell policies from more than one company. Just as premiums can vary widely from company to company, commissions paid to agents on various policies vary quite a bit. If the policy an agent is suggesting does not seem to be the best fit for you in some ways, it's perfectly fine to request alternatives.

Increasingly, satisfied consumers are bypassing the agent scenario altogether and buying insurance online. You can get quotes instantly from any number of sites and obtain quotes from several companies simultaneously so you can compare prices and review company ratings. It's a good idea not only to review ratings, but to look at when a company was founded. You may not want to buy insurance from a company that was founded last year. There are many venerable and aged institutions to choose from if this helps you feel more confident in the product.

Ch. 7

Resources

• Smart Money offers a useful worksheet to help you figure out how much coverage you need. In addition, you'll find a glossary of life insurance terms, a comparison of term and whole policies, and suggestions for saving on life insurance: www.smart-money.com/insurance/life

• Get an instant quote for term life insurance at: www.reliaquote.com. This site also offers a needs analysis worksheet.

• To compare quotes on term insurance from several companies simultaneously, go to: www.intelliquote.com.

• For more information about disability insurance: www.about-disability-insurance.com. This is an educational site with many useful links and articles.

Insurance Quotes

Company Name	Quote	Notes

Ch. 7

Assets List

Institution/ Investment	Account Number	Approx Cash Value ($)	Death Benefit ($)	Phone	Website	Sign in	Password	Date of Purchase
ABC Bank		2,000	——	1-800-xxx-xxxx	www.abcbank.com	jdoe	1234	

Ch. 7

Estate Planning:
Attorney Referrals and Information about Services

When you call attorneys and ask some initial questions, consider asking about:

- Fee structure

- How many times they expect you will meet and where the meetings will take place

- The services they offer

- What the timeline for completion would look like (how long this process takes, start to finish)

1. Attorney name: _____

   Contact information: _____

   _____

   Referred by: _____

   Fees: _____

   _____

   Services offered: _____

   Notes: _____

   _____

Ch. 7

1. Attorney name: _____

   Contact information: _____

   _____

   Referred by: _____

   Fees: _____

   _____

   Services offered: _____

   Notes: _____

   ....

1. Attorney name: _____

   Contact information: _____

   _____

   Referred by: _____

   Fees: _____

   _____

   Services offered: _____

   Notes: _____

Ch.
7

Personal Finance: Money Matters for the Growing Family

During the months when you were expecting, how many times did you hear the words "your life will change forever"? As you now know, it's true; there isn't an aspect of life that is left unchanged by the birth of a baby and the financial realm is no exception. Your financial picture just shifted to include another person. It's likely that your spending practices and the way you allocate money will change, whether you actively intend it to or not. It's not easy to recognize even dramatic shifts in spending and this section is about making your spending patterns and tendencies more transparent for you.

Babies aren't necessarily expensive at first. Although they require some start-up purchases with big price tags (cribs and car seats, clothes, and an endless supply of diapers), baby-related expenses are actually modest over the first few years, especially when compared with the expense of raising older children. On the other hand, the temptation to spend has never been greater. You have an outrageously adorable baby to shop for! You spot irresistible clothes and must-have toys all over town. What's to rein you in?

When you become a parent, it's a great time to examine your financial habits and do some planning to accommodate the new person in your life. Whether it's new paint for the nursery, a contribution to your college savings plan, or sports equipment for your Little Leaguer, you will continually invest in your child. This section offers you a tool to figure out how you spend your money now and determine how much extra money, or disposable income, you have at the end of the day or month or year to spend on your little one. This will ultimately help you project what you can afford to spend on baby gear, baby supplies, and baby impulse buys.

"Daily Income" Method

Wait— don't turn the page yet. I know you're skeptical. Let me be candid with you: finances have never been my thing. In a world in which opposites often attract, I had the good fortune to marry a financial tour de force. I'm going to explain how to get a handle on expenses in just 28 days and I promise it will work for even the most finance-phobic person. This method, described below, changed the way I look at the flow of money and has been a great help to me and others who have tried it. If perhaps you are one of those enviable people who find it easy to live within your means and you have a workable budget already up and running, pat yourself on the back and take five.

What's so great about this exercise? Why will it be worth your toil? Most books that talk about budgeting ask you to log expenses for 30 days, put them in categories like housing, food, etc., and then add them up. Next you subtract the monthly expense total from your monthly income. That method will only get you so far because it tells you by how much you are in the red or the black. But chances are, you already know if you are steadily increasing your credit card debt. (Red bad, black good.) The exercise outlined for you here turns this on its head by looking at what you spend in the context of what you earn while you're earning it. This method, which we'll call the daily income method, begins with the money you have on hand instead of ending up there, only to find you have too little. You will learn by how much you are over (or under) spending and see how this technique can help you make changes in your spending habits.

Step 1: For our purposes, we need a number you have probably never crunched before: your daily income. It's actually very simple to calculate. Locate your most recent pay stub, find your after-tax earnings or take-home pay after any other deductions, such as an automatic withdrawal for

Ch. 7

savings, and divide by the number of days in the pay period including weekends. The number of days in your pay period will likely be seven, fourteen or thirty-one. If you and your partner share expenses, add your daily income totals together and make sure you both record all purchases on the worksheet. It's only for 28 days. If you can parent together, you can do this together.

Step 2: Let's say that your daily combined take-home income is $100. To make this exercise more illustrative throughout the month, we're going to break out the biggest expenses first and average them over 28 days so several days or weeks aren't skewed by a big expenditure, such as paying your rent or mortgage. To do this, divide your housing costs by 28. For example, if your monthly rent or mortgage is $1,550, divide it by 28 and you find that your housing cost is $55 per day. This leaves you with $45 per day ($100 total less the daily cost of housing) to spend on other things and 45 is going to be your daily income number, the number you'll work with for 28 days.

If you have another large monthly payment, such as a car payment, that you prefer to factor in in advance, feel free. This principle holds true for a yearly payment such as homeowner's insurance too. Divide the yearly payment by 12 (to break the sum into a monthly figure) and then divide that number by 28 so you can factor it into your daily number, if you wish.

You will record what you spend each day and some days it will be much less than your daily income—if you only buy a latte, for example. Other days it will be astronomically higher; perhaps you'll pay all your bills on the same day of the month. It doesn't matter because your spending will be averaged over a month's time. Don't fret about spending more than your daily income on any given day but notice if you spend more than that for several days in a row. This exercise is initially to see how much you're spending—and on what—and then it can be repeated later and used to scale back

Ch. 7

spending if you feel the need to do that.

Each column in the chart will begin with your number at the top. Each purchase should be recorded using a dollar amount and a short description. Writing the amount

this idea to a larger sheet of paper and use one sheet of paper for each of the four weeks. When I tried my hand at budgeting I hung the paper on the inside of a kitchen cabinet so that it was in easy reach—with a bit

Sun	Mon	Tues	Wed	Thurs	Fri	Sat	Total
$45 (25) groc (15) Movie	$45 (30) phone (40) DSL	$45 (30) sitter	$45 (15) dry-cleaning	$45 (55) gym membership (20) diapers	$45 (5) lunch	$45 (40) groc	
Total: 5	Total: (25)	Total: 15	Total: 10	Total: (30)	Total: 40	Total: 5	$20

of purchases in parentheses can be helpful and in the world of accounting anything in parentheses indicates a negative amount, or subtraction.

To get the total for the week you add up all the positive numbers in the daily totals, which in this example add up to $75 (5+15+10+40+5=75). Then subtract all the daily totals in parentheses and you'll find you're up $20 for the week (75-25-30=20).

Record as many purchases as you need to for each day. If you don't have enough space, either write in the margins or simply transfer

of privacy—and I updated it daily. When a new week rolled around I taped a new sheet over the old ones so I could collect a month's worth of expenses all in one place.

The above is not a wicked math problem to torment you, but actually a very satisfying way to get a handle on your expenses during a time when expenses often increase and income often decreases. If this appeals, give it a try. You don't need to start on the first of the month because the worksheet is organized by day of the week. You could even start today. . . .

Ch. 7

Daily Income Logs

....

sun	mon	tues	wed	thurs	fri	sat

Find this worksheet online at www.babyfilebook.com

notes: _____

_____

Ch. 7

Daily Income Logs

sun	mon	tues	wed	thurs	fri	sat

Ch.
7

notes: _____

_____

Daily Income Logs

....

sun	mon	tues	wed	thurs	fri	sat

Ch.
7

notes: _____

_____

So, how are we doing? Hopefully, that was helpful, if not enjoyable. If you are satisfied that your spending is what you thought it was and all is well, there is no need to repeat this for another four or five weeks. If you ended the month in the hole and you want to use this chart as a way to curb spending, repeat as many times as needed. The practice of entering your daily purchases and seeing them against your daily income can have a subtle inhibiting effect and can be a quick fix for overspending. After two or three cycles you won't need this tool anymore because you will know where the limits are and you will have a concrete understanding of how much disposable income you have to play with during each month.

Step 3: At this point you can put your monthly total to work if you choose. One useful next step to take with this information, even just one month's calculations, is to review your purchases and see how much you spend on baby-related items. For example, you may want to have one large category called "baby," or you may want to break it into several subsets, such as childcare, baby supplies, and baby luxury items (DVDs, toys, etc). Go through the chart and write a letter next to each baby purchase, such as "C" for childcare. Then you can tally it up and find out how much you spend per month on baby-related expenses.

If this is your first baby, these will obviously be new expenses for you. If your monthly total was negative, you can look at which baby expenses are necessary and which fall into the luxury category. Then you can decide what else in your life needs to give to accommodate the necessary baby expenses. Use the space below for notes or calculations.

Before we leave the world of personal finances, I want to add a caveat about this daily income method. While it can tell you many important things, such as whether you are spending more money than you're earning and even what you're spending it on, it is not a big picture tool. And in this business of

Ch. 7

babies, you really have to look at the big picture sometimes. There's nary a family who can afford every baby-related expense at one time. These costs probably have to be spread out over several months. You can use your monthly total from the daily income exercise and multiply it over several months to see what you might have on hand in a given six-month or year-long period.

Other things to consider are expenses that occur annually, such as property tax, and seasonal expenses like Christmas. The daily income method is again limited in this regard. If you feel after doing this exercise that you are not saving and planning for expenses adequately, in either the short term or the long term, this is a great time to meet with a financial adviser to get a savings plan together. Some advisers charge by the hour and it may be a good investment to spend a few hours with one to get things on track for the long haul.

You can use the "big picture" worksheet to look ahead to upcoming expenses and see what you'll need to save to cover them.

Resources

Books:

- *Making the Most of your Money* by Jane Bryant Quinn

- *Just Give me the Answer$* by Garrett, et. al

- *Get a Financial Life: Personal Finance in your Twenties and Thirties* by Beth Kobliner

Websites:

- College savings calculators and other tools: www.savingforcollege.com

- CNN Money: www.cnnmoney.com. Go to personal finance, where there's an excellent section called Money 101.

- Yahoo personal finance: www.yahoo.com

- Quicken personal finance software: www.quicken.com.

Ch. 7

Projected Big-Picture Expenses

Projected Baby-Related Expenses*:

*For typical costs, see Chapter 1 on nursery set-up and baby gear

Description   **Dollar Amount**

_____   _____

_____   _____

_____   _____

_____   _____

_____   _____

_____   _____

Subtotal   _____

Other Big-Picture Expenses

Use this space to try to project expenses such as payments on a car, investments in a college savings plan, a vacation, etc.

Description   **Dollar Amount**

_____   _____

_____   _____

_____   _____

_____   _____

Subtotal   _____

Total Projected Expenses   _____

Ch. 7

Appendix

APPENDIX

Baby's Milestones: A Record of Firsts

The First Time Baby...

Smiled _____

Cooed or squealed _____

Reached for/grasped an object _____

Laughed out loud _____

Slept through the night _____

Rolled over _____

Ate solid food _____

Recognized his/her name _____

Got a first tooth _____

Sat without support _____

Crawled _____

Waved goodbye _____

Stood _____

Walked _____

Danced _____

Spoke a word _____

Said "Mama" or "Dada" _____

Got a haircut _____

Took a trip or vacation _____

Celebrated a holiday _____

Ch.
A

Baby's Healthcare Record

Pediatrician

_____   _____
Name   Address

_____   _____   _____
Phone   Fax   Email

_____
Health insurance company and policy number:

_____
Pharmacy phone number:

Ch.
A

Office Visits (or phone calls to doctor)   Date: _____

Concerns and questions: _____   **Notes:** _____

_____   _____

_____   _____

_____   _____

· ·

Office Visits (or phone calls to doctor)   Date: _____

Concerns and questions: _____   **Notes:** _____

_____   _____

_____   _____

_____   _____

· ·

Office Visits (or phone calls to doctor)   Date: _____

Concerns and questions: _____   **Notes:** _____

_____   _____

_____   _____

_____   _____

· ·

Office Visits (or phone calls to doctor)   Date: _____

Concerns and questions: _____   **Notes:** _____

_____   _____

_____   _____

_____   _____

Ch.
A

Office Visits (or phone calls to doctor)   Date: _____

Concerns and questions: _____   **Notes:** _____

_____   _____

_____   _____

_____   _____

Office Visits (or phone calls to doctor)   Date: _____

Concerns and questions: _____   **Notes:** _____

_____   _____

_____   _____

_____   _____

Office Visits (or phone calls to doctor)   Date: _____

Concerns and questions: _____   **Notes:** _____

_____   _____

_____   _____

_____   _____

Office Visits (or phone calls to doctor)   Date: _____

Concerns and questions: _____   **Notes:** _____

_____   _____

_____   _____

_____   _____

Ch.
A

Office Visits (or phone calls to doctor)   Date: _____

Concerns and questions: _____   **Notes:** _____

_____   _____

_____   _____

_____   _____

. . . .

Insurance Claim and Medical Billing Notes

When you make calls to your insurance company or your doctor's office,
it's a good idea to keep track of the date, the name of the person you spoke with,
and any next steps or resolutions to pending claims.

Growing by Leaps and Bounds

Baby's Growth Record...

Date	Age	Height	%	Weight	%

Ch.
A

Immunization Record

Allergies to Medications: _____

Immunization	Date	Age	Reaction, if any
Diptheria, Tetanus, Pertussis (DTP, DTaP, DT)	1.		
	2.		
	3.		
	4.		
	5.		
Polio (OPV, IPV)	1.		
	2.		
	3.		
	4.		
	5.		
Measles, Mumps, Rubella (MMR)	1.		
	2.		
Hemophilis Influenza (Hib)	1.		
	2.		
	3.		
	4.		
Hepatitis B (HBV)	1.		
	2.		
	3.		

Ch.
A

Immunization	Date	Age	Reaction, if any
Varicella (Varivax)	1.		
	2.		
	3.		
Influenza	1.		
	2.		
	3.		
	4.		
Other			

Screening Tests

Test	Date	Results
Lead		
Hearing		
Vision		
HCT (Complete blood count)		
HGB (Hemoglobin)		
PPD (Tuberculin Skin Test)		

Ch.
A

Resources

• For a list and description of the vaccines required by your state, visit the National Network for Immunization Information web site: www.immunizationinfo.org

• At the Centers for Disease Control and Prevention web site, parents can print immunization schedules based on their children's birth dates and gather information about immunizations: ww.cdc.gov/nip

• The Vaccine Adverse Events Reporting System allows parents to report reactions or side effects of immunizations: www.vaers.org

Solid Food Record for the "Older" Baby

Use this sheet to record new foods tried and any reaction that might indicate a food allergy. Most doctors advise waiting until a baby is between 4-6 months of age to begin solids.

Date	Food	Notes

Ch. A

Emergency Numbers

Poison Control: 1-800-222-1222

	Name	Phone 1	Phone 2
Parents			
Relatives or Neighbors			
Doctor			
Dentist			
Alarm Co.			
Veterinarian			
Pharmacy			

Ch.
A